Embracing The Grind

By: Justin Goldman and Mike Valley

Published Independently by: Justin Goldman and Mike Valley
Cover Art Design by: Carl Herring

 This book was co-written by Justin Goldman and Mike Valley. All content included in this manuscript is original literature produced by the two authors. Discussions held with the NHL goalies and coaches took place during the 2016 calendar year.

First Printing: November, 2016

ISBN-13: 9781537721736
ISBN-10: 1537721739

We would like to extend a very special thanks to the following goaltenders and goalie coaches for sharing stories from their personal lives: Ben Bishop, Fred Brathwaite, Scott Darling, Jhonas Enroth, Johan Hedberg, Jimmy Howard, Mitch Korn, Drew MacIntyre, Curtis McElhinney, Evgeni Nabokov, and Jordan Sigalet.

TABLE OF CONTENTS

Preface
Live, or Die Trying

A near-death experience is both a blessing and a curse.

Blessed to still be alive, you revel in the five senses, never again taking them for granted. To see, taste, touch, or feel anything at all is a gift that brings a tinge of timeless euphoria to every moment thereafter. You have an instant love for everyone and everything, all while gaining a newfound respect and appreciation for Nature and the endless connections between people, places, things, and time.

But as blissful as it sounds, you can never escape its curse.

Forever plagued by that eerie out-of-body moment, you're left with a permanent scar of severe emotional distress. Unsure if you were meant to live or die, you struggle to cope with the psychological impact. There are days when you think the world is out to get you, so you can't bring yourself to fully trust anyone or anything. You even distance yourself from friends and loved ones, lest you leave them with the same curse.

This fear leads to social anxiety, because so much of your focus is spent battling the paranoias that become permanently lodged in the back of your mind. You never want to face the fact that something like this could potentially happen again, so you drown out the dark thoughts and flashbacks by staying as busy as possible. You find comfort in isolation, and over time, you start to feel estranged.

All four of my near-death experiences were harrowing moments that I dare not wish on any man or foe. Three of them transpired before the age of 12, which was right around the same time I realized goaltending was quietly coded into my DNA. Having narrowly survived each time, I'm eternally grateful for all these blessings and second chances in this life, yet I'm destined to fend off the curses for the rest of my days.

We've all gone through some scary moments in life, so we can agree on one thing: No matter how much it hurts, you must face your demons every day and find a way to embrace the grind.

With the support of 11 NHL goaltenders and goalie coaches, Mike Valley and I have once again joined forces to help others — not just goalies, but all people — overcome the toughest of times. Whatever fears you're currently facing and whatever your personal grind may be, this book is here to help you fight the good fight.

Due to my unique relationship with Death as a teenager, I went through high school knowing all too well that sooner or later my luck would run out. In late-2000, during my freshman year of college, my worst nightmare came true when he came knocking on my family's door once again.

Riddled by a withered mind and a lengthy battle with Parkinson's disease, my grandfather chose to take his own life with a shotgun to the head. Nobody expected it, nobody knew he had a gun, and nobody was prepared for the aftermath. Reeling from the shocking news, it was the unmistakable finality and stark permanence of his suicide that left me hollowed to the core.

The moment Death waltzed right up to our front door and whisked my grandfather away, my mother's otherwise peaceful and loving side of the family was ripped to shreds. Anger, blame, resentment, and backstabbing raged on for weeks and months, leaving my father to deal with most of the messy aftermath. Real life and death, or what I thought I knew of both, knocked me completely senseless. I just couldn't bring myself to care about most things anymore, and for a while, that included hockey. Instead, I took a long draw from the cup of college life, experimented, partied, and hid my pain.

At my grandfather's funeral, I remember averting my eyes as his casket slowly sank into the ground. Still angry and confused by his selfish act, my gaze shifted away from the gravesite and directly onto a large stone sepulcher standing 10 yards away. As I silently swore an oath to never visit his grave again, I was able to decipher a string of words etched onto the marbleized cover of the massive tomb:

"Death and life contended in that combat stupendous."

In that moment, the archaic quote made perfect sense to me.

Live, or die trying.

Like many of you, I use music as a compass to help guide me through some of life's most difficult times. Fuel for the soul, music creates a certain type of energy inside your body and mind that has the power to transform thoughts into actions, dreams into reality, and ideas into results. Whether you're coping with the loss of a family member or simply need to escape the daily grind, music is like an invisible best friend, one that's always there to push you forward and bring you closer to your destiny.

It was on December 18, 2015 when I discovered a new band that had an instant profound impact on my life. Reeling from a gut-wrenching stretch of misfortune over the previous two weeks, I found myself stuck in a mire of depression. Bad memories from the moments I shared above consumed my mind as I neared a point of no return. Onward I traveled in a downward spiral, unable to control the spinning and lacking the bravery to discuss my issues with anyone.

I couldn't rely on a friend or family member to fully understand what was going through my mind, so I had to suck it up and face the fight alone. So inward I turned, and with music by my side, I faced the grind head-on.

Mere seconds into hearing ***Shylmagoghnar*** for the first time, all of the unhappiness and desolation started to melt away. Their music traveled down my spine and through my entire body, which took my mind off my past problems and thrust me into the current moment. Their debut album *Emergence* packed such a potent burst of inspiration that it instilled me with the strength I needed to simply let go of all those negative feelings weighing me down. Their music literally freed me from my own troubled mind.

Based in the Netherlands, ***Shylmagoghnar*** is comprised of two close friends, *Skirge* and *Nimblkorg*. As mysterious as their names sound, there's no mistaking the piercing honesty and spellbinding threnodies of their music. It clearly isn't for everyone, but as a lifelong fan of the metal genre, I think they strike a perfect chord and balance between the realms of light and dark, good and evil, aggression and romanticism.

Above all others, the song *"A New Dawn"* resonated with me the most. Enraptured by the mastery of this lyrical tapestry, it became the ode to my life's struggles. From the death of my grandfather to all four of my near-death experiences, I cherished the way the song spoke to me about those times of desolation. The sheer strength of the song's symbolism reached out and touched me to the point where I broke down on more than one occasion.

As Christmas Day approached, the song became the genesis of a new creative spark. Suddenly, my pen attacked paper with vicious resolve, and less than 10 months later, this book now stands as a testament of sorts to their influential work. In fact, *Skirge* and *Nimblkorg* went on to play a very significant role in the structure of this Preface, so it is through their guiding hands that I wrote the words of reflection below.

Furthermore, it is an honor to have their blessing to publish the song's lyrics, so I hope you will take a moment to contemplate what they mean to you and your own personal grind. By doing so, it will not only reinforce the purpose of this book, but it will bring some well-deserved recognition to their brilliant music.

SHYLMAGOGHNAR - A NEW DAWN

We are men of a thousand faces
of the motionless mask.
Underneath which a battle is raging
and danger lies in losing grasp.

We must burn our boats to leave behind
the shores of our damnable past,
as we take a deep breath through the fog
that used to suffocate.

What's done is done, the dice were cast
and the only path before us lies
striding towards the riches of a new dawn.

But before we can relinquish
the strangleholds of the past,
we must one last time revisit
those depths, where we hardly dare go.

Enter the mind!
A bottomless pit of inspiration.
A bottomless pit of sorrow as well.
One must watch his steps
not to fall in self-deception.

Oh! Where we once gave in
to endless waves of melancholy.
The weight of the world
and the torment of troubled souls.

There is no turning back now, to what once was.
As hardship transformed, the path has been forged
Pain led to knowledge and insight!
So revel while you can in the dusk of the past
as a new dawn; grand, rejuvenous
emerges through our hands.

Revel ye pity humans, in the dusk of the past
as a new dawn emerges, emerges
through our hands!

Therein lies hope. Therein lies strength.
Built on the ashes of the old world.
Therein lies life; therein lies meaning; therein lies strength,
as the sun of a new dawn engulfs the skies!

As a goaltender, you carry a hefty burden on your shoulders. Others may not see it, but you've chosen to face an extensive amount of pressure as the last line of defense. Because of this, you're forced to battle your own mind on a daily basis. Self-doubt, the ebbs and flows of your confidence, the constant fear of failure, and the frustration attached to the physical beat down is like a torrential downpour of highs and lows. If you cannot exhibit great mental control and emotional stability, the position can lead you to a very dark place.

For these reasons alone, you must always be ready to embrace the many "new dawns" a goalie is destined to find. That "new dawn" could be the start of a new season or junior career, getting traded to a new team, setting loftier goals, returning from an injury, or even rebuilding your entire game. Goalies face myriad new dawns in different ways, but it is through all of these experiences that you grow, evolve, and improve.

The stark duality between *A New Dawn* and goaltending is quickly triggered in the song's second line.

"Of the motionless mask..." refers to the most sacred and iconic piece of goalie gear, the mask. It draws parallels to that of a medieval knight in armor, wearing an impenetrable mask that can withstand any sword or shot. Similarly, every goalie looks a little different with their unique colors, designs, styles, and custom setups, but they all swear the same oath and face the same pressures. So when that motionless mask goes down and the battle on the ice ensues, goalies everywhere become the *Men of a Thousand Faces*.

The battle a goalie endures is then referenced in the next line. *"Underneath which a battle is raging..."* could be interpreted as all the struggles that you face throughout your playing career. These struggles are often so personal that they're hidden from the media, teammates, family, and friends. As a result, goalies *"lie in danger of losing grasp..."* on their reality. Always working to define themselves — like playing style and purpose — goalies are prone to losing a grip on who they really are and where they want to go.

The *"...shores of our damnable past..."* can be seen as all of your negative and solemn past experiences. Whether it was something that happened on or off the ice, symbolically, it is everything you strive to forget. It is all the bad goals against, the terrible losses, or something more unfathomable, like the loss of a loved one.

"Enter the mind!"

It most certainly is a bottomless pit of inspiration and clearly capable of being a bottomless pit of sorrow as well. Like all people, goalies have to deal with a cacophony of scars, visible and invisible, from their past. Instantly, Clint Malarchuk's ongoing fight with depression after his ghastly injury with the Buffalo Sabres comes to mind. And do you think Ondrej Pavelec has ever been the same since his scary collapse on the ice way back on October 8, 2010? Not a chance.

Of all the symmetry I find in this song, however, this next line is the ultimate clincher:

"One must watch his steps not to fall in self-deception..."

Since goaltending is a daily grind within your own mind, I believe is one of the most damaging and detrimental parts of the process. No matter hard you try to avoid deflecting blame onto others, making excuses for your mistakes, or lying to yourself about what you're doing, sometimes there's simply no escaping it. You have to be disciplined and exhibit sheer will in order to be as honest as possible. But I know that this is never easy when you face such lofty demands.

For this reason, you must be extremely careful not to fall into a pit of lying to yourself. You can't cheat the game, because if you do, you're only cheating yourself. It isn't easy, but you can't hide certain feelings and you can't avoid confrontation just so you can feel better. Don't run away from the grind, turn and embrace it!

"Where we once gave in to endless waves of melancholy..."

Fighting the highs and lows of an 82-game season is the epitome of a melancholy wave. Goalies often face way more bad stretches than good, so in order to make it to the pro ranks, you must be able to ride that wave no matter what. From a goalie's perspective, there's no denying that *"...the weight of the world..."* often rests on the shoulders of legends like Patrick Roy, Martin Brodeur, Grant Fuhr, Carey Price, and Henrik Lundqvist. These guys are expected, no, demanded to take their teams to the Promised Land. Failure is not an option, so be rest assured that their souls have gone through plenty of tormenting stages in their careers.

"Pain led to knowledge and insight!"

For all goalies, the scars you collect symbolize growth and perseverance in sport and in life. They may come back to haunt you like ancient demons from the past, but you still have to covet them all, because they bring wisdom, much-needed experience, and the confidence needed to survive future scars.

I believe the final two stanzas go without saying, as the hope, the meaning, and the strength you gain from the past brings more purpose to our futures. That purpose, no matter how you ultimately achieve it, is exactly what you need to push through even the worst of grinds. Treat your battle scars as a source of inner strength.

Throughout that week of Christmas, I continued to study ***Shylmagoghnar's*** lyrics to the point where I felt an overwhelming urge to contact the band. On a wing and a prayer, I introduced myself through a Facebook message, thanked them for their creation, told them my idea for this book, and kindly requested any additional insights into the meaning of the song. Knowing that musicians usually like to leave songs open to interpretation, I never expected to hear a response, especially since they lived in the Netherlands.

To my amazement, not only did I receive a response on Christmas Day, but over the course of writing this book, they shared a number of personal insights into their music. This resulted in a new friendship, one that was built from afar, but one held extremely close to my heart. After a few short conversations with *Skirge* and *Nimblkorg*, I was so excited to find that, despite our vastly different lives, we had a few things in common. Namely, it was a passion for personal growth within our fields of study.

At first, I was tempted to publish a majority of their responses. But after sharing an earlier version of this Preface with them, I decided to include only a few key insights. Some interpretations, no matter how accurate or vague they may appear in your eyes, are simply meant to remain unknown. As *Skirge* said to me, we often see the lyrics to a song as a mirror; what stares back at you is exactly what is looking into it.

It was extremely tough to narrow everything down, but I had to share the line below from *Nimblkorg*. When speaking candidly about one part of the song, he said:

"'There is no turning back,' because you cannot truly commit to something before you give up the option to abandon it."

I loved this, because if you aspire to be a pro goalie someday, you have to accept the fact that you can never abandon the journey. If you're still willing to take the plunge in search of your pro goaltending dreams, then you must do so knowing that the journey will consume all of you. It could even reach the point where it drives you mad, pushing you right to the edge of your sanity.

The other piece of insight I wanted to share had to do with the line about the motionless mask. In a heart-felt discussion with *Skirge*, he revealed to me that this line was not about strength or endurance, but about the masks we wear and present to the outside world. When we do this, we show nothing of what we really are.

Goalies not only wear masks on the ice, but as people in our everyday lives, goalies are often programmed to show no emotions at all. Over time, you get used to hiding your face, your expressions, and your feelings, because to exhibit despair, anger, or frustration is to lack a sense of unwavering discipline that all goalies need. We are expected to be even-keeled at all times, a blank canvas with no sign of happiness, weakness, or pain. As a result, part of the grind is dealing with this constant lifting and lowering of the emotional veil that accompanies the goaltending position.

Skirge summed it up perfectly when he told me, *"The mask is both something that helps and hurts."*

It may seem unrealistic to expect someone to live this way, but every goalie knows that how they act when the mask is on can oftentimes bleed into their day-to-day lives, and vice-versa. It's not as simple as flipping a switch on and off. Sometimes it's difficult to leave hockey at the rink, and sometimes it's hard to leave all the worries you face in life behind when you enter the rink. It takes time, internal fortitude, and great patience to truly learn how to compartmentalize both sides of the coin.

Truth be told, this comparative analysis between goaltending and the song could be a book all of its own. For now, however, I think I've made enough connections to move on. This part of the writing process was one of the most motivating experiences of my life, and I can't even begin to express how grateful I am for the friendship both artists have offered to me.

In closing, I want you to think about one final connection.

Shylmagoghnar went through 10 long, arduous years of training and evolving their music theory and composition techniques before painstakingly creating their impeccable debut album. The same can be said for the pro goaltender, who spends 10 years grinding it out in juniors, college, and then the minors before they are fully ready to have success in the NHL.

So if you're reading this at age 18, get used to the fact that life won't look anything like this when you're 28. And if you're reading this at age 28, you better believe life is going to be so much different when you're 38. A lot of wonderful and terrible things may happen to you between now and then, many of which will completely blindside you and knock you off your feet. But regardless of how your path unfolds, realize that sometimes you will rise, sometimes you will fall, and whether you like it or not, you will find different ways to embrace it all.

Now that you've been primed for the book's introduction chapter, ask yourself this all-important final question:

"What does embracing the grind truly mean to me?"

If you don't have a definitive answer yet, then I hope this book will help you find one as you read on. I also hope that you can better appreciate just how hard these

NHL goalies and goalie coaches worked to survive some of the toughest grinds imaginable, including depression, injury, failure, and even alcoholism.

More importantly, I hope you notice how none of them wanted to change anything that had happened to them, good or bad. Their gratefulness for the opportunity to be playing a game for a living cannot be lost in the mix, because being grateful is precisely why they are still happy amidst the pressures they face. Similarly, you must also be willing to trudge through all of that which grinds you down. For no matter how hard you work, no matter how much talent you have, and no matter how much luck you get along the way, nothing worth fighting for comes without pain and sacrifice.

Over the past decade, I have compiled a small library of motivational quotes aimed at supporting and inspiring goalies. There are some gems waiting to be discovered in this book, but one of my personal favorites is, *"The battle is never truly won or lost."*

I think this quote perfectly encompasses the goaltender's grind, because there's never a point in time when you've truly mastered the position. When you're winning, you're only as good as your last game, so you have to focus on what comes next. When you're losing, while it may damage your pride, you still took a step forward in your overall development. Without quality doses of both, you will never reach your full potential.

So may all of your greatest victories be short-lived and all of your toughest defeats be quickly forgotten, for as it goes in goaltending and in life, you must embrace the grind in order to rise again.

- Goldman

Introduction
Defining the Grind

Whether you're a goaltender, a coach, an athlete, or doing something completely different with your life, you've probably heard these quotes many times before:

"When the going gets tough, the tough get going."
"What doesn't kill you only makes you stronger."
"I'm just plugging away, trying to grind it out."
"Time to rise and grind!"

In today's troubling times, sharing phrases like these act as a great rally cry for all of humanity. No matter what you're going through in life, whether it's a battle with depression and loneliness, or a global issue like economic and environmental strife, these morsels of wisdom remind us that we're not alone. No matter the color of your skin, the country you're from, or the beliefs you hold closest to your heart, every one of us shares in the infinite highs and lows of this bizarre and fascinating world we live in. *Everyone has difficulties of their own and everyone is fighting some kind of personal battle.*

Truth be told, there are people all over the world that are facing way more treacherous struggles than the average athlete. For those who have or want a profession in the world of goaltending, however, this book is dedicated to the unique struggles we face in the crease and behind the mask. If you're not a goalie, we hope you will stick with us. Many of the lessons in this book could apply to you as well.

The goaltender's grind is special — it's an all-encompassing lifestyle that the position demands. From the intensive training to the mental toughness to the discipline of your daily routines, embracing it means enduring a lifetime of different emotional, physical, and mental adversities. Great success as a goaltender does not come without great sacrifice of body, mind, and spirit. We're biased, but there are very few positions in pro sports that challenges one's physical and mental limits as much as goaltending.

Subconsciously, goaltenders swear a silent oath to embrace the grind. If you love playing the game of hockey, you do so knowing that it will strip you of many qualities of life. It will be physically dangerous, and in some instances, even life-threatening. It will also be emotionally dangerous, as it can spiral you into depression, cause you to develop anxiety, and even bring out strange obsessive-compulsive disorders you never knew existed.

Despite the torture and strain goaltending places on the body and mind, you still choose to be a team's last line of defense. From year to year, game to game, and practice to practice, you choose to fight a never-ending battle. It rages inside the mind as much as it does inside the rink, and even though it hurts at times, you do it for the sheer love of playing the game of hockey.

To continue introducing you to the book's theme, we wanted to share our individual definitions of embracing the grind. Everyone has a different way of explaining it, which is part of why this subject is crucial for the goaltending community to discuss as a whole.

Valley: *"Embracing the grind is your ability to accept a hard-working lifestyle. Then it's working your butt off day in and day out and doing everything you can to push yourself forward. It's putting up with all the crap that is thrown your way — more than you ever imagined — while still staying positive and getting better. It's embracing each day with a smile on your face. It's never questioning why you are on this journey, even though everyone around you thinks that the smartest thing you could possibly do is quit and live a normal life. It's re-defining your work ethic in order to improve. Eventually, the grind becomes you, it's all you know, and it's the only way you know how to live. You then realize that, regardless of what challenges or obstacles you face, life is not about the elusive goal you're chasing. It's about loving what you do every single step of the way."*

Goldman: *"Embracing the grind is the never-ending fight against your mind, body, surroundings, and emotions. It's the lifelong process of developing the skills needed to play and live at your best on a daily basis, no matter the cost. As it goes with all walks of life, whether in success or in failure, we learn the same lesson: Goaltending is a battle that is never* *truly won or lost. That means you must exhibit great discipline of mind, body, and spirit – despite all external forces working against you – for the betterment of your team. It's having the ability to tune out everything beyond your control while maintaining an unwavering confidence in yourself. But being yourself also means steering clear of self-deception. It's so easy to trick yourself into working less than 100-percent, so embracing the grind, in simple terms, means never cheating the game and never cheating yourself."*

Knowing that everyone goes through their own struggles, this book (which is a follow-up to *The Power Within*) sheds some valuable light on the elite goaltender's grind. We did this by interviewing 11 former and current NHL players and coaches in different settings, diving deep into their minds in order to discover what "the grind" really looks and feels like. We also strived to highlight each individual's pursuit of a dream, how that dream was threatened in different ways, and how they overcame those challenges. Fortunately, we were left with a special collection of wise insights, uplifting messages, and candid stories of failure, personal strife, and beating the odds.

We then supported the 11 interviews by adding short, co-written chapters aimed at giving you some simple lessons on how to embrace the grind. Whether it's detaching yourself from results or truly cherishing your friendships in hockey, these little morsels of wisdom act as mantras for goaltending and life. They go hand-in-hand with the interviews and complete what we hope will be another timeless book on goaltending.

While some important life lessons were revealed in each interview, a resounding theme of courage radiated throughout the entire book. For the goalies, true courage was not just pushing through the daily bumps and bruises, but also working tirelessly towards something they really wanted but had no guarantee of getting. Even with this permanent fear lodged in the back of their minds, they all welcomed defeat with resilience and accepted failure with humility. Their answer to embracing the grind, therefore, was simply meeting the days where they lacked motivation, inspiration, and energy with the resolve and discipline to still do whatever it took to accomplish their goal for that day.

This book also revealed another vital lesson about the daily struggle: The truly elite goalies never consider "the grind" as a negative thing. No matter how tough it may have been for them, they knew the grind played a vital role in building them up and creating the blueprint for their future success. Setbacks were an integral part of ney and played a central role in the quest they took to achieve their wildest dream.

After you've read the final page and life carries on, we hope you will have gained a little more appreciation for the bad times you face as a goaltender. They're just as important as the good times, and in many instances, even more important. Furthermore, we hope you will realize that, no matter what may be bothering you at the current moment, most likely, it won't even matter in the long run.

Above all things, we want to leave you with one final point.

Goaltending should be something you love to do, even when it's not fun. Everything you cherish about the goaltending experience should come from the love of taking every step of the journey, not just realizing the dream of the final destination. So if you're ever feeling down, want to quit, or struggling with self-doubt, just stand tall, stay strong, and use this book to help you grind it out!

Chapter 1
JHONAS ENROTH

Introduction: *The smallest goaltender in the NHL has been on quite the remarkable 10-year journey. He's been through seemingly endless strings of recalls, reassignments, and quirky backup situations. He's fended off numerous naysayers and survived the major pendulum swing towards bigger goalies in the late 2000's. He also went on a 6-0-1 tear in relief of a concussed Ryan Miller to help send the Buffalo Sabres to the 2011 Stanley Cup Playoffs. He set a new NHL record when he earned his first three wins by way of a shootout, including a barnburner in Montreal's sacred Bell Centre. He even carried his country to a Gold Medal in the 2013 World Championships on native soil, Sweden's first victory feast in a shocking 26 years. Yes, we speak of none other than the persistent and intelligent Jhonas Enroth. This is the same goalie who, despite all of his great accomplishments, once went more than a full calendar year without a single win. Despite the torture he went through during that time, it also brought him the wisdom and experience he needed to continue the ride with Dallas, Los Angeles, and now in Toronto, where all-new obstacles and challenges surely await him.*

Goldman: You must have developed a pretty thick skin over the years due to so many people talking about your lack of size. I know we've talked in the past about size being overrated, but how hard was it for you to establish yourself as a legitimate pro goalie in North America?

Enroth: "Actually, until I was 18 years old, I never thought about it as being a smaller goalie [laughing]. But when I was in my draft year, that's when people suddenly started saying I was too small. I remember it was kind of shocking, because I never thought about that or heard it in Sweden. Until then, it was just about stopping the puck. I didn't know you had to be big to be good at goaltending. But like you said,

I've been dealing with that since I was 18. It's been hard at times, but today I think I'm fine. I honestly think that when I give up a goal, not often it's because I'm not big enough. If you're a big guy, you might have a little more self-confidence; that's natural. So you definitely have to work on your confidence a little more if you're smaller. You really have to trust yourself. I feel like I've been proving to myself that I can play well at this level, especially when I do things the way I know I can, and the way I should be."

Goldman: So when I say the term "Embracing the Grind" and we look at what you've had to go through in your career, aside from size, what's the first thing that comes to mind?

Enroth: "I actually went through an entire calendar year without a single win. I wasn't playing a game every day and it stretched through the lockout, but I still probably lost 10 or 12 straight over the course of two seasons. All of the media and fans made a big deal about that fact, so it was definitely the toughest time in my career. But I got through it, really grew from it, and took away a lot of lessons from the experience. I remember how, in the last couple of games before breaking it, I was just trying to not care so much about the score and focus on trying to play my game. It's easy to say and very hard to do, but that's what I did right before I finally won a game again. But that was definitely the toughest stretch for me in the NHL."

Goldman: Most goalies would agree and understand how much harder it is to push through something like that when you're only playing sparingly. Can you talk more about how you were feeling or what you were going through during that tough stretch?

Enroth: "Well, you're definitely lacking in confidence when you don't win for a while. But you just need to focus on how you feel on the ice during games and practices. When it comes to the game, you almost want to try and approach it like a practice. I'm able to stay pretty loose in that regard now, and I think I react to plays and shots better when I don't think too much. That's the hard part when it comes to playing games during a long losing streak; you get caught thinking too much and you get too nervous. During that time, I actually worked with a sports psychologist and she really helped me.

She always told me to try and imagine the game as a practice, and one way to do this was by thinking about how the ice is just ice. It doesn't matter if it's a full house or an empty practice rink — what happens on the ice is the same. So that helped me get through that tough stretch. You have to focus on working hard in practice, and when you don't overthink, that hard work translates right into the game."

Goldman: In a few of these interviews, some of the goalies expressed that one of their biggest frustrations was dealing with the many misconceptions that come from the media and fans. During your tough losing streak in Buffalo, how did you continue to stay positive and push through all of that?

Enroth: "You definitely have to detach yourself from it. You can't read too much into what the media and fans are saying. I was fortunate to have Ryan Miller next to me in Buffalo, and I saw how hard he worked every day, so it was pretty easy for me to realize I just needed to work at least as hard as he did in practice. I just kept telling myself that it was going to turn around soon, and trust me, I know that's easy to say and so much harder to do. We know it's hard to stay positive when things are rough, but it's so huge when you can actually find a way to look at things positively and just live in the moment. You can't drift away too much into the future or get caught thinking about what happened in the past couple of games."

Goldman: Now that you've been through these types of things, what would you say to your 20-year-old self if you had a chance to sit down across from him at a dinner table?

Enroth: "I think that's an easy answer. I'd just tell him to try and enjoy it more. I would want to be a bit more relaxed when I was younger, especially when it came to games. I was too uptight on game days and I wasn't really used to playing in NHL games or performing every night like I was in the minors. I was pretty uptight my first year, so I'd probably just tell myself to enjoy it and relax. That's something I've been able to do more in my career now that I'm a little older."

Goldman: You mentioned earlier that you learned a lot about embracing the grind from Ryan Miller. What about with Jonathan Quick? He's

had his fair share of injury issues the past few years and still plays so many games. What have you learned from him?

Enroth: "I definitely learned what he does to figures out how to manage all of his different situations. He's very inventive. His instincts are pretty amazing, because he just goes out there and stops the puck, even if it doesn't always look like he's doing it the right way. He's a guy that can play loose every game. It's obviously easier to do that when you've won two Stanley Cups, but what I've been learning from him this season is how loose and relaxed he is when he plays."

Goldman: You were the first goalie in NHL history to win his first three games by way of a shootout. I clearly remember when it happened. You were called up from Rochester one morning, only to play later that same night against the Canadiens in Montreal. It was another classic sellout, and it was in just your second or third NHL start. How did you battle the nerves for those three games?

Enroth: "I just kept telling myself that it was just another game. Obviously that's not the case when you come up from the AHL to play at the Bell Centre, but we had a pretty good team at that time, so I remember getting a lot of help from them. For me, the key was believing that it was just another AHL game and then trying to block out everything around me. The shootouts were fun — I've always been pretty good at them — and we had some really good shooters, so it wasn't too hard to win those games, honestly."

Goldman: During those darker days in Buffalo, I know you were victimized by one of the league's worst defenses. How hard was it to manage that aspect of the grind when you were so desperate for just one win?

Enroth: "It was tough, because I'm kind of a hockey nerd. I like to follow hockey and I take pride in my own game. So it was definitely tough, but as a goalie, you have to start educating yourself about different ways to stay positive. I actually did this by reading "*The Power Within*" shortly after you guys published it. That was one way to do it on my own, and I know I said it before, but you also have to find ways to stay positive on your own."

Goldman: Reflect back on that. You're trying to stay positive and your team is fragile. What are you doing off the ice or before the game to get you into that positive mindset?

Enroth: "I guess it starts by trying to feel good in practices and morning skates — just trying to stop your teammates as much as you can. Then you have to try and carry it over into games. It's hard to put into words, but I definitely remember how tough it was to do. At the time, I also had good help from Miller and Jim Corsi. I've been going through a pretty tough stretch this year too, actually, with the Kings. It's been difficult for me to find a good consistent level when you don't play as often as other guys. It's a similar situation for me right now in L.A., just as it was behind Ryan in Buffalo. I'm going through that grind again right now, but I'm much more mature about it compared to a few years ago. I've found more ways to relax and think about other stuff."

Goldman: I love that you're being so open and honest with where you're at right now with the Kings. What are some of the ways you relax? How do you strike that balance between not thinking about hockey 24-7 and then flipping the switch when you do get to the rink?

Enroth: "I try to talk a lot with my friends and family back home. When I talk to them, I don't really think too much about hockey, because we talk about normal, everyday life. I think that's a good thing to do, especially if you're from Sweden and your friends are back home. I'm not sure if they've noticed that I will talk a lot more with them when I'm grinding it out [laughing], but that's one thing I do. Speaking to your family is important as well, and I've learned that it's way easier to get your mind off hockey when you're at home. On the road, it's all about hockey, because you're always with your teammates or you're alone in the hotel room just thinking about games. At home, you have your everyday routines with your girlfriend or wife and kids. You don't want to go through a tough stretch on the road, but if you do, just talk to your family."

Goldman: Let's talk about winning the Gold Medal at the 2013 World Championships. That had to have been a huge confidence-booster amidst those dark days in Buffalo.

Enroth: "It's good that you brought that up, because I think that's when I played the best hockey in my pro career so far. I had that tough stretch where I didn't win a game for over an entire calendar year hanging over my head, but I managed to win a couple of games and ended with an over .500 record during my time in Buffalo. Then I came over for the World Championships and I played in my hometown, so I actually got to see my friends and family after practices and team events. I didn't think too much about hockey — I just went in there and played. I think that's where my career turned around. Since I won a Gold Medal, I definitely think I've been a better goalie. I learned from that tournament that I'm way better when I'm more relaxed. I didn't think about the consequences of losing, I just played and reacted and our team really did well."

Goldman: It's a different type of pressure though, playing for your home country, right? You were more comfortable at home, but did you still feel pressure that caused you to worry a little bit?

Enroth: "We definitely had pressure, but I remember that it was just very fun to play in that tournament at home. Hockey was really fun at that time. There have been times when hockey wasn't very fun, and that's when you usually have a bad stretch. For me to play well, I need to have some fun with it and be relaxed. That's a huge key for me. Don't think too much, just trust my instincts."

Goldman: I think it's so important for readers to consider that in their own game. When hockey isn't fun, how do you still find a way to compete? You can't just stay in bed all day and hope the motivation will come. You have to create your own luck.

Enroth: "I think it helps to remember the good times, because I was always having fun playing when I was growing up. It's when hockey became a job that it started to be way less fun at times. But it's a job we have to do, so you pull yourself up off the ground and try to appreciate where you are and what you have. When hockey's not fun, I just appreciate the fact that I'm actually in the NHL. There's a lot of people that would love to be here, so I cherish the little things. I make sure to enjoy doing all those things that make up my daily routine in the NHL."

Goldman: Did that come from your parents? Did they keep it fun for you growing up?

Enroth: "My parents never put any pressure on me. It was all about having fun. It was my own choice to play goal and they supported me every step of the way, so I've been very fortunate to have them. My parents have been great and they are obviously the biggest reason why I've been able to have the success I've had."

Goldman: I remember the season where Ryan Miller was going through a lot of tough off-ice stuff in the first half, and then went off the grid during the All-Star Break. All of a sudden, he tore it up down the stretch. There were some articles written how he basically took a mini-vacation to clear his mind. Do you remember that? How important is it for you guys to take those breaks during a season?

Enroth: "I think it's huge, especially if you've been struggling. Get away from it all, think about other stuff, and then start fresh after the break. I wasn't in Buffalo full-time when that happened, but I think the biggest key for him was the chance to just hit the reset button. You can break those last few months down into smaller segments and just try to focus on that, like the way I think during a game. I take games in five-minute spurts and the season in five-game segments. Break things down into shorter periods and just try to do well in each of those short periods."

Goldman: How about dealing with locker room chemistry? How tough is it to get along with guys that aren't necessarily getting along with other teammates?

Enroth: "I think every team has their own problems. There are 25 guys trying to win every night, so everyone can't always be friends all the time. I think that's why it's so important to have a strong leadership group that pulls everyone together and can get everyone to pull their weight and move in the same direction at the same time."

Goldman: I guess you have plenty of experience joining a new room with Buffalo, Dallas, and then Los Angeles [and now Toronto]. What was the transition like for you going to Dallas? Was it pretty smooth or did you hit a rough patch?

Enroth: "It was both, actually. I was moved a few weeks before the Trade Deadline, but I didn't want to leave Buffalo. I felt pretty comfortable there and I felt like it was my team and my town, so I was upset when I got traded. By the same token, when I came down to Dallas, I was really excited to be there. It was a really good experience because they obviously have a great team there, and I was able to see how a different organization worked. I got a chance to work with Mike, which was great, too. I had been following him a little bit; it's been pretty interesting to read the things he talks about, so I was very excited to work with him. So it was both tough but exciting. It was a crazy experience, but I'm happy I had it. I grew from it. I grew as a goaltender and as a person. I'm just so happy I had that experience."

Goldman: Let's wrap this up by giving you a chance to speak directly to readers. What's your advice on the idea behind this phrase — a phrase that I feel encapsulates your career to date: Always Learning.

Enroth: "It's very important to always try and get better. It doesn't matter if you just had a shutout the night before, you should still try to get better the next day. My drive is to always try and stop more pucks than I did the day before. As long as I can remember, that's something I've always tried to do, whether it's in practices, games, or whatever it might be. Everyone at this level has that drive, and that's why we all are here. That's why we have been able to embrace the grind for so many years. The guys that didn't make it, well, they probably didn't have quite the same drive. Having the fire to get better every day is very important for young goalies."

Chapter 2

Detach Yourself from Results

"If one dream should fall and break into a thousand pieces, never be afraid to pick one of those pieces up and begin again." - Flavia Weedn

As young goaltenders, we all choose a path that forces us to spend most of our lives striving for a single goal — to win the Stanley Cup. Whether it's a wild pipe dream or eventually becomes a possibility, we are bound to struggle with the idea that the ultimate outcome is the opposite of what we truly desired. It is such a rare feat that failure is almost inevitable.

To know that you will probably fail to reach your dreams and still commit your life to trying anyways is a sign of true courage. And with true courage on our side, we can embrace any grind. But a part of being courageous is being able to embrace the idea of Detachment, a powerful tool that will help you gain perspective and see the bigger picture.

In goaltending, there is a special and mysterious paradox. The harder we try for something, often the harder it becomes to achieve. It's only when we're a little older and a little wiser that we start to let go of the results, and that in turn is what we need to relax and achieve our goals.

With that paradox comes the realization that acceptance is a major part of detachment. If you put too much pressure on yourself to perform, you spend more time worrying about your image and the anxiety that comes with being seen as a failure. This is a vicious cycle that can lead to a downward spiral of self-doubt and an all-consuming obsession with your image. Accepting life's inevitable failures will help you realize that you may not be as talented as you think you are. It is usually when a goalie reaches this point that the worry and anxiety begins to subside.

Trapped somewhere between a win or a loss, even the best goaltenders in the world still spend a lot of time worrying about success and failure. So much of who they are is defined by their performances and results. They face so much pressure to win and so much strife when they lose that this calling can sometimes reach the point of total consumption, which is never healthy, no matter how relaxed they may think they are.

So break free from the chains of your outcomes, look beyond the veil of the stats, and forget about the opinions and judgements of the media and other meaningless pundits. Always strive to keep yourself in an even-keeled state of mind, because one of the keys to successful goaltending is always being able to live in the moment. The less you worry about the future, the better you will be able to focus on the present and execute your game plan.

If you struggle with letting go of results, try taking a deep breath and realize that hockey is a team sport; you are not the sole reason for wins or losses. Failure as a goaltender, especially in just one or two tough games, does not make you a failure at life. It does not make you a loser socially, either. It just makes you more tried, tested, and true. It makes you, you!

Chapter 3

Ben Bishop

Introduction: *Not only was Ben Bishop cut by the same USHL team that drafted him, but scouts and skeptics alike said he was simply too tall to play and compete in the NAHL. Since then, Big Ben has done nothing but prove them all wrong. After a successful championship season with the Texas Tornado and a solid tenure with the University of Maine Black Bears, Bishop spent four years paying his dues in the American Hockey League before finally breaking into the NHL with the St. Louis Blues. From there, despite two trades, untimely injuries in the Stanley Cup Playoffs, and being the backbone of a growing franchise with rising expectations, he has become Tampa Bay's career leader in wins and saves, as well as a Vezina Trophy finalist in the 2015-16 season. It certainly helps to be blessed with the gift of size, but that doesn't mean it's any easier to handle the pressure of being a starting NHL goalie. It took nearly 15 years for Bishop to finally realize his loftiest dreams, and heading into the 2016-17 season, the battle is only getting tougher. But through everything he has faced in his career, it just goes to show you that it's not the size of the body that matters most, but the size of the heart.*

Goldman: I'm always amused when I look at your background and realize we both spent our senior year of high school playing hockey in Dallas, Texas. But growing up in St. Louis at the time, what was your journey like leading up to that year of junior hockey in Texas?

Bishop: "I remember going to a Blues game when I was really young and telling my dad that I wanted to be a goalie. But nobody in my family played hockey, so I just took some lessons and played for fun. Never in my wildest dreams did I ever think about playing in the NHL as an actual profession. It was more like one of those fantasies you thought about all the time, but never expected to actually happen. I just rode that wave until high school, and even up to that point, I never really knew much about AAA or junior hockey. I was pretty uneducated about the whole hockey process, because there weren't that many people from St. Louis going on to play juniors or college in the first place. So I was just playing for fun when I got drafted into the NAHL. I didn't even know that there was a draft or anything like that! I think someone told me the next day that I had been drafted by Texas, but I didn't even know who they were [laughing]."

Goldman: Not even aiming for junior hockey at the time you got drafted is pretty hilarious. Youth sports is such a different animal these days.

Bishop: "At the time, I knew more about the USHL than the NAHL. When I got drafted by the USHL team, I was like, 'I guess I'll go try out and see what happens,' but didn't really know much about the whole thing. I went up there and tried out, didn't make the team, and then I was told to go play in Texas for a year and go from there. So my dad did some research, I went to the Tornado, and it ended up being one of the best years of my life. Like you said, I lived in Dallas for my senior year of high school and some of the best friends I've ever made were from there. I was still pretty naive, though; I didn't know what to expect and didn't know if I would be the starter. I battled it out with the other goalie, I ended up with the starting role, and I never looked back. We had a great season and we won the NAHL title, while that team in the USHL went through a bunch of different goalies that season."

Goldman: From the time you started playing youth hockey in St. Louis until the time you made the NAHL, did you ever really feel any type of actual pressure as a young goalie?

Bishop: "I would say absolutely zero. I never looked at hockey as a tryout or anything like that. There weren't many other hockey goalies around at the time, maybe like two others in all of St. Louis. So it was all just for fun, and I think that made the ride all the more enjoyable."

Goldman: Looking back on that now, do you think playing strictly for fun during those years, without any pressure from your parents or other external forces, helped you embrace all of the new experiences playing junior hockey, thus having more success?

Bishop: "Absolutely. There's no doubt about it. I think now you see kids getting a bit more burned out, or as they get older, their careers tend to dwindle, because they're pushed and pressed way too hard. I think I was the complete opposite. It wasn't until I got to juniors when I first started to really take hockey seriously. Before that, it was all just fun and games."

Goldman: Was being cut from the USHL team your first 'bad' or upsetting hockey experience?

Bishop: "I think I tried out more for the experience. It was more like, let's just go out there and see what happens. If I make the team, I make it. If I don't, I don't. I didn't really feel too much pressure. It was my first time going to a real hockey try-out, so if it didn't work out, I knew I could just go back to St. Louis and keep playing there. College hockey wasn't even on my radar, so I didn't feel any pressure there, either. It's never fun when you get cut and it puts you back in your place a little bit, but I knew I was going down to Dallas for the same kind of tryout process, and obviously I made that team and everything worked out."

Goldman: Well now I'm curious. When *did* you feel pressure of any kind for the first time?

Bishop: "When I made the Texas Tornado. The other goalie was a newcomer as well, so I didn't want to go down there and be a backup to a rookie. I went full-tilt down there, and that's when the competitive nature really came into play. I think I got a shutout in one of my preseason games, played well the first few games of the season, and then took over from there."

Goldman: If that's the case, I'm guessing that was the season where you first started to realize what the physical grind was all about.

Bishop: "I remember the first month went by and we were winning a lot, so everything was going really well. Then one day my coach came up to me and said I was on the Central Scouting list for the NHL Draft. I had no idea what kind of opportunity that would turn out to be, so it was like a, 'Whoa, maybe I can play in college and actually make it to the NHL...' moment. After that, I really started to take things more seriously. The working out, the approach to the game, trying to be more focused, playing in every game; I just wanted to put more importance on everything."

Goldman: Is that when you started developing that laser focused pre-game mentality?

Bishop: "To be honest, I don't know exactly when I developed that very intense game day attitude. You know from our time together in Madison the past few years that I'm a pretty fun-loving guy during those practices and off the ice. But in games I'm pretty intense. I guess it started down in juniors in Texas and then I carried it with me to Maine and then into the pros."

Goldman: I've seen first-hand in Madison how hard you guys truly work to prepare for an NHL season. It's also amazing to see how you guys can flip that attitude switch so quickly. You go from 100-percent relaxed to 100-percent fierce in an instant. How do you explain that ability? What is it inside of you that allows for it to happen?

Bishop: "It's definitely something you develop over time. I've come across some guys that take it to an extreme, though. They spend the whole day in this really serious mindset and have all these different or goofy routines. I try and stay away from all that. For me, it's simple. When you have such an enjoyable job — I'm playing a sport for a living and making good money doing it — you practice, you get prepared, and you get ready to win a hockey game. That's what you're getting paid to do. So that's what allows me to have that intense attitude during those times. It's like when you're studying the night before a big exam and you go really hard. You punch the clock. Well, when you only have so many games in a season and each game is only a few hours a night, you can be 100-percent into it. That's the time for me to punch the clock. As goaltenders, if we make a mistake, nobody's backing us up when the puck's in the back of the net. If you're on the road with 20,000 people cheering when the red light goes on, you have to be really focused. If you're joking around and you're not 100-percent serious, it's a lot easier to make a mistake. It's like driving in the snow. If you're not paying attention or you're talking on the phone, you're more liable to get into an accident. But if you have two hands on the wheel and you stay focused on the road, you're going to be a lot safer. That's like my game day. I have both hands on the steering wheel and I'm 100-percent focused."

Goldman: I know you said your time at the University of Maine was pretty smooth sailing, but what about the transition to the pros?

Bishop: "There's definitely a lot more to handle when you turn pro, especially when you're playing in the minors and you're trying to break into the NHL. That's when it really feels like you're just grinding it out. In college, you play a couple of games on the weekend, compared to playing three or four times a week in the AHL. That's where you're playing three games in three nights, your team is tired, you're on a six-hour bus ride, and then you have to play the next night and get lit up. That's when you get agitated, mad, and you realize it really is a tough grind."

Goldman: Any AHL experience you remember in particular that sticks out as being especially difficult?

Bishop: "Definitely my last year in Peoria, because I was banking on making the Blues. But when I didn't make it and got sent down, I had one of those, 'Why am I doing this?' moments. You're pissed off and you're young, but I look back on it now and think it was all a key part of the experience. There's definitely moments where you wonder if it's ever going to happen. You have to get lucky, to be honest. Unless you're a top draft pick that's given a real opportunity, you have to get some luck. Somebody usually has to get hurt for you to get a chance to play in the NHL. It's an elite position where there's only 60 total spots in the whole world, and there's a lot of people in the world trying to be an NHL goalie. So you have to get lucky to some extent and really stick with it. You have to hope for a chance and be willing to wait for that chance."

Goldman: Let's talk a little more about that moment when you didn't make the Blues. What made it a key part of your journey and how did you feel when it happened?

Bishop: "I just felt like I was ready to play in the NHL that year, but I didn't get the opportunity I deserved. It was one of those moments in my career where,

.'e than anything, I was super mad. I wouldn't even say I was disappointed. I was more pissed off. But I went down to Peoria with the attitude that I was just going to dominate. Every game was going to be a tryout for 29 other teams, because I wasn't really worried about making the Blues anymore. I wanted to get other teams to trade for me. Having that type of attitude really changed my career, because I played extremely well in Peoria and when the Trade Deadline came up, Ottawa wanted me. So for me, I was at one of those crossroads where you can either feel sorry for yourself or just suck it up. I went down to dominate in the hope that someone would trade for me. That's the approach I took to get through it."

Goldman: It's one of those 'easier said than done' situations I'm sure, so how did you manifest that positive attitude in the midst of such a frustrating moment?

Bishop: "It was tough. When I first went down, I didn't want to be there. The first week you're more disappointed than anything, but after that, you rally behind yourself and you get to work. You can sulk or you can step up, and after that week went by, I realized sulking wasn't going to do me any good. It wasn't going to change my situation. I was still going to be down in the minor leagues, so it was more about embracing a different type of opportunity and grind."

Goldman: When you were traded to Ottawa, it seems like that's when doors finally opened up. I can remember watching you in some of your first and only games with the Blues and then seeing you in Ottawa, and you looked like a totally different goaltender.

Bishop: "It was a good opportunity for me and I felt happy with where my game was at. When I got called up from Binghamton, it wasn't much of a grind at all. I just went out there and did it. I played well when I was put in, I stuck with it, and it was the same kind of thing as in Peoria; I was playing for all 30 NHL teams and Tampa Bay was the one that showed interested in me."

Goldman: Once you established yourself with Tampa Bay, that success led to higher expectations. How were you able to embrace more

pressure from the nauseating media and loftier expectations from the organization? How did you grind that out long enough to become an NHL All-Star?

Bishop: "I think that's part of the whole process. You see some of the younger guys come in and they have to go through all of that to make it to the NHL. You might be a little young or naive, so you don't necessarily understand everything that comes with it. I had been in the American League for three and a half years, and then I was a backup in Ottawa for over two years. So I think I had a better grasp on what it took to handle the media and play night-in, night-out at a high level. When I got to Tampa, I felt like all of that experience was an advantage for me. The lengthy process had paid off, because when I finally got the opportunity, I knew what it took and I was ready. I honestly don't think there was much of a grind beyond that. I knew what to expect out of myself, the schedule, the team, and the media, so I was able to just go out there and not have to think about it too much. It's just part of the whole process; juniors, college, minors, backing up in the NHL, and then the opportunity to be a starter. You learn how to handle all of that over the years."

Goldman: Let's say you're sitting at a table, and across from you is a 23-year-old Ben Bishop. What would you say to yourself about this crazy pro hockey experience you're about to embark upon? What advice would you give yourself on a personal level?

Bishop: "That's an easy one. In my first full year in the AHL, I got called up like two weeks into the season. In my first start for St. Louis, we won 4-0, but I ended up leaving the game in the third, because I slightly pulled my groin. But I played again a few weeks later in San Jose and did really well. At the time, I thought, 'Oh, I'm ready for the NHL' [laughing]. I had been a pro for two weeks, not even a full month, and I thought I was ready to be an NHL goalie [laughing]. Looking back on it now, I would definitely tell my younger self that I am nowhere close to being ready. I had so much learning and maturing to do at that age, so I'd also tell myself to stay patient and keep learning. You think you're ready at a young age, but really there's so much more to learn — both on and off the ice — about how to handle it all. I think a lot of younger guys think they're ready because they have all the tools, but that's only half the battle."

Goldman: What's the most frustrating or difficult aspect of being a full-time NHL goaltender?

Bishop: "I think it's the fact that there's a lot more that goes into it than most people realize. They see you go out there and either play good or bad, but I don't think people realize all of the stuff that goes on behind the scenes, and what it really took to get there. They think you're living a good life and everything's great, but they don't realize all of the hard work and sacrifice needed to get to where you are today. So maybe it's the misconception people have of who you are. I don't think people realize the grind you really have to go through. Not every night is going to be a Picasso [laughing]. I think that's what I've also learned about embracing the grind. You have to learn how to deal with the fact that there's going to be good games, bad games, good stretches, bad stretches. Just try to stay on an even level where, if you have a couple of bad games, you don't get down on yourself. You have to realize that you're going to have bad games and stretches where things just aren't going well, or you're not feeling great and getting victimized by bad bounces. That's part of the grind and part of the maturation process you face over the years. You have to learn how to ride both waves and not get too high or get too low."

Goldman: Is there one phrase or mantra that you say when things are really tough?

Bishop: "Yeah, I actually learned something from Ed Belfour when he was my goalie coach for a couple of months in Peoria. It was a short stint for him, but I actually learned quite a bit. He said when things aren't going well, you should go back and watch some of your highlights and best saves. Get that good feeling back, have those good memories and good thoughts brought back into focus. Pop in an old game tape where you played really well, and now heading into your next game, you're seeing and thinking about some of your best saves, instead of thinking about the last game. Now you have good recent memories instead of bad ones."

Goldman: That's a great tip. In order to really push through a lot of the stuff that grinds you down, you just have to remember that you're in the NHL for a reason.

Bishop: "Yeah, absolutely. Look back at those games and say, 'This is why I am who I am today. This is what I do well.' I mean, there's going to be tough stretches and that's true in anybody's profession, so you should always try to go back and look at the good times. I think that's true with good teams, too. All the good teams I've ever been on have had good chemistry. Guys are having fun, getting along, and everything's happy-go-lucky. I mean, it's probably the case with most things. Happy wife, happy life type of thing. I don't have a wife yet, but I hear that all the time [laughing]."

Goldman: That's funny, because we interviewed Brian Elliott in "The Power Within" and he actually talked about how getting married helped him realize that he had a real life outside of hockey. He said that it improved his life balance and helped him grind it out in Colorado and St. Louis.

Bishop: "Those first years in the minors, you're just a kid. You don't have too much going on and so much of your life just revolves around hockey. When you can put hockey on the back-burner when you're not at the rink and not think about it so much, I think it helps quite a bit. You have to find a hobby other than hockey to help keep your mind away from it when you're not at the rink. That way when you're there and preparing, you can focus on it 100-percent. But if you're thinking about hockey 24-7, when you're at the rink, it's no different than at home. When you can get your mind off hockey and not worry about it all the time, it definitely helps."

Goldman: The Lightning have a really talented young Russian goalie in Andrei Vasilevskiy, and I think he might be going through that exact type of grind right now. Do you see shades of your past in his present?

Bishop: "I've gotten to know him pretty well over the past few years and he has all the tools, but like I said before, it's so much more than just having the skill. You also have to be able to handle the ups and downs. He has always been a number-one guy and has always excelled, but this year he went through a stretch where I think he lost five in a row and things weren't going well. It's tough to learn at his age. Obviously he'll get down on himself, but you have to realize it's a long season. If you win a game 6-5, you can't get mad at yourself. You need to realize that you have to win at all costs. You don't get paid to lose 1-0 and then skate off happy just because you played well.

cess to be learned. You want to play well every single night, but at this earn how to handle the nights where you have to grind out a 6-5 game. o be just as happy with a 6-5 score as a 1-0 score, because a win's a win. It's a tougher thing to learn as a younger kid, because you just want to play well every game, and for the most part, you *think* you can. But that's not going to happen at this level. So he's probably learning this first-hand and going through that process right now. He's going to be a really good goalie, there's no doubt about that. But he still has that maturity process to go through."

Goldman: Like you said earlier, having the tools is just half the battle.

Bishop: "How many goalies get drafted in the first round and don't pan out? You have all these tools and you're used to being the best and always playing well. Then you get hit with a reality check if you don't know how to handle it. Everyone in the NHL has the tools to stop the puck. It's the other half of being able to embrace all of the different grinds that go along with it. You just have to keep learning how to handle the wins and the losses."

Goldman: I think what I love about the title and theme of this book is that "Embracing the Grind" is something we can all relate to. I also think it gets people thinking about their work ethic. If you enjoy working hard, you'll almost always be able to grind it out.

Bishop: "That's part of the process, too. For a goalie, if you're the first guy at the rink and the last guy to leave, if you're working out every single day, and if you're working hard on every single shot in practice and always going 110-percent, you have to try and remember to work smart, too. Just because you work hard doesn't necessarily mean it will translate into you eventually being the best goalie. You have to find out what works for you. If you practice every single day, obviously you can't go 110-percent all the time, so you have to figure out when you need to dial it back. What kind of shots do you actually need? When do you need time off to take care of your body? I think you really need to learn what your system is and what makes you successful. Know when to throttle down a little bit and figure out what works best for you. Everyone works differently, so going 110-percent 365 days a year isn't the right recipe for everyone. You have to find what works for you."

Goldman: That parlays nicely into my next question, which has to do with self-management. I mean, it's really only a tough grind if you're over-working and putting too much pressure on yourself. You still have to go out there and have fun. It's just a game.

Bishop: "If your life as a goaltender turns into a real tough grind, then you're not going to be a happy person. If you feel like every day you go in, you're not happy or in a good mood and embracing it, that's probably the toughest battle you will face. You have to enjoy it and you have to love it. And if you're going to the rink every single day, you have to know how to handle the times when you're not enjoying it."

Goldman: It's all about balance and having a purpose to everything you do, and that's kind of like a form of discipline. There's the physical work, but then there's the work you put in to master your mind and your game plan. Like you said, it's finding your recipe. It brings this interview full-circle, because we already talked about your ability to strike that balance between being totally dialed in and still relaxing and having fun.

Bishop: "When I was in Peoria, there was one year where I wanted to be the first guy in the rink and on the ice and the last guy to leave every single day. I wanted the coaches to think I was the hardest worker, so I did that for a whole year, and I remember it was a really tough grind. I was waking up an hour earlier every day, but by the time the next season rolled around, I had realized that if I got an extra hour of sleep every day, I would be more rested and therefore more successful. So while I wasn't the first guy at the rink anymore, I was away from the rink just enough to keep my mind off hockey a little more, and that really helped me. So it's just a lengthy process, because back then, I just didn't know. The first few years ended up being way more of a grind than it was enjoyable, and as a result, I wasn't as successful. But by my fourth year, I realized what I needed to do to strike that balance."

Goldman: I think that's a great way to wrap things up. It almost sounds like your solution to the grind is to embrace is so simple — love to play and strive to strike a balance between fun and hard work. I know a lot of younger U-12 and U-14 goalies and parents will read this book, so I think a good closer would be to reflect on your parents. Can you explain why their hands-off approach was so important growing up?

Bishop: "My dad didn't play hockey and my mom didn't have a hockey background at all, so in their eyes, even to this day, I've never played a bad game before. I was never once criticized by my parents for anything hockey related, because they didn't know or necessarily care about it. They were always on the supportive end. They never pushed me or signed me up for camps I didn't want to attend. They were just purely supportive. They were my biggest fans and it really helped. They didn't have unrealistic intentions of me being an NHL goalie. It all just kind of happened. Letting me just be me was a huge, huge benefit to my career."

Goldman: You were able to just go out there as a kid and naturally develop your own skills. Nothing was forced, you just evolved naturally. That's why it continues to be a dream come true for you.

Bishop: "Especially as a kid, hockey was never a grind. It was always just something I wanted to do. We'd play a little bit of hockey in the summers, but I was also playing baseball, basketball, tennis, and golf. That made me a better goalie. You can't play hockey year-round."

Goldman: And since your parents weren't hovering over rinks and courts and fields when you were playing all those different sports, it allowed you to develop self-awareness at an earlier age. You learned through sheer trial and error how to better manage your own attitude and emotions within the realm of competitive sports.

Bishop: "Part of that was because my parents never knew the game of hockey, but it ended up working out great. To this day, regardless if I call them after a good game or a bad game, they're always the same. They're never critical or upset. Your parents are usually the people you talk to the most throughout your career, and they also have the biggest influence on your life, so you often take their same approach. When they're not down on you, you're not going to get too down on yourself. You hate to see parents who are too critical of their kids, because first and foremost, young goalies need to be having fun. You have to enjoy the game, but if you don't enjoy it because you're being pushed too hard by outside sources, it's not going to be a good experience. That's not just in hockey, but with everything in life."

Chapter 4
Trust the Process

"Life is an ever-flowing process and somewhere on the path some unpleasant things will pop up – it might leave a scar, but then life is flowing, and like running water, when it stops it grows stale. Go bravely on, my friend, because each experience teaches us a lesson. Keep blasting because life is such that sometimes it is nice and sometimes it is not." - Bruce Lee

The goaltender's path is never paved in gold. It's full of sudden twists, turns, trenches, and hidden doors along the way. So how do you learn to deal with the vast amount of life's unknowns?

By focusing on what you can control, working as hard as you can every day, and trusting the process. You'll need some luck and help along the way, but if you can do those things, you should sleep better at night knowing you're chipping away and doing everything you can to achieve greatness. Trust yourself, have confidence in the path, and it will all unfold as it should.

We also know that it's much easier said than done. But nothing worth fighting for comes easy, which is why we dedicated an entire book to the concept of embracing the grind.

In fact, having complete faith in your decisions, especially when your future depends on so many little steps and big moments, will be one of the most difficult emotional battles you will face as a goalie. Whether you're dealing with social acceptance, your teammates, or your style of play, you're going to spend a lifetime learning how to worry less and just go with the flow.

Inevitably, the sooner you realize that it's a muddy, murky, dirty path to travel, the sooner you will come to terms with the mistakes, the failures, and the wrong 'l not go the way you expected. Games, friends, and opportunities acrifices will have to be made. Your body will suffer short and long-term pain. You will have regrets.

But if you have the unyielding inner confidence to trust the process, whatever happens along the way won't really matter. This inner confidence, often recognized as blind faith, is something innate and deeply spiritual that fuels your dreams and aspirations. You will desperately need this throughout your journey. If others view this cockiness or arrogance, continue to strive for balance and try to maintain a quiet ego along the way.

Regardless of the obstacles, and some face more than others, a single truth remains: The only constants in life are adversity and change. So trust that everything that happens to you — even the little things — is playing a key part in manifesting a successful and bountiful future.

Did you just have one of the worst practices in your life? Trust the process. Are you feeling totally uncomfortable in brand new gear? Trust the process. Were you benched after giving up three fluky goals in a big game? Trust the process. Are you retooling your game after recovering from off-season hip surgery? Trust the process. Are you dealing with the fallout of having a bad attitude a few years ago? Trust the process.

A big part of trusting the process is not just realizing your path will include pitfalls, but accepting the mistakes you've already made. You need these grinds in order to achieve what you so desperately desire. If there is no pressure, there can be no diamonds.

So learn to trust that the time you're putting in will lead you to bigger stages. Never back down from a challenge, never stray from the path you're on, and don't shy away from tough situations. Accept and embrace them, for they will refine your character and purpose. Keep going when it hurts the most. Keep fighting when you've already been beaten. Keep learning when you think you've learned it all.

With every single save you are sowing a seed, but those results won't immediately be seen. For it's not the destination that truly matters, it's the journey.

Chapter 5
Curtis McElhinney

Introduction: *Within every goalie's mind, there's an inherent identity struggle. Bouncing from team to team, city to city, and goalie coach to goalie coach, a part of you is always chasing and changing life in order to adapt and thrive in your new home. The color of your team's jersey, the design of your pads and mask, and the style of your play paints a raw picture of what you encompass as a goaltender and who you are as a person. So when Curtis McElhinney suddenly went from being the successful leader of a storied NCAA D-I program at Colorado College to the sparsely used backup to Calgary Flames legend Miikka Kiprusoff, the battle to create a new identity began. Transitioning to a "solid and reliable" backup didn't happen overnight, however, as Curtis, ready and thirsty for more playing time, was eventually traded to Anaheim, Arizona (still Phoenix at the time), and then Columbus. It was there that he finally discovered the secret elixir needed to create his true NHL identity. It didn't come easy, as McElhinney was sidelined for close to eight months after suffering an atrocious and bizarre pelvic injury. After pushing through the turmoil of the lengthy recovery process, the fire to continue his NHL career burned brighter than ever before. The Blue Jackets took notice right away, and since then he has stood as a flag bearer, taking great pride in supporting Sergei Bobrovsky while also mentoring Joonas Korpisalo and the rest of their young goalies.*

Goldman: I know this is the first time we've ever talked, but it certainly won't be the last. These interviews are kind of like a little bonding experience, and I know they have also been pretty therapeutic for a lot of the goalies Mike and I have interviewed.

McElhinney: "The best part for me now is that I'm not starting out on my NHL career, I'm on the downswing. So it's all gravy at this point for me now [laughing].

I'm not caught up in all the stressful stuff like I was when I was 24. That can be a little overwhelming for some people."

Goldman: How was it when you were 24 compared to where you are right now?

McElhinney: "When you first start out, your only objective is to make it to the next level. You have this one-track mind where you think you'll get there right away. Next thing you know, you go to your first NHL training camp thinking that, if you play well in your first exhibition game, you're going to somehow make the team. But I don't think most people realize that they want experience. The reality is that they want you to play a lot of games, and you're probably not doing that the first few years in the NHL. Some do make that jump, but those are your truly elite guys. I think that was the biggest wake-up call for me. Regardless of how well I played in training camp, the reality is that they [the Calgary Flames] wanted me in the minors playing games. That was a little bit of a wakeup call to pro hockey."

Goldman: Did that challenge hit you pretty hard emotionally as a pro rookie?

McElhinney: "It wasn't necessarily a negative thing. It was a good first year for me to get a taste of it with the scheduling, especially coming from college. The change of pace and everything else certainly led to an adjustment period; there was a little bit of growing up that needed to be done. So those first two years I'd say were good years. The first year was a really big challenge. I had some good games, had some bad games, and had a lot of interesting experiences with my coaching staff. But learning how to be a professional hockey player was the most challenging part."

Goldman: Aside from the pace of the game and the travel, what was the most difficult mental or physical adjustment you had to make during those first two years in the AHL?

McElhinney: "Getting ready to play on a nightly basis. I was used to a situation in college where if I had the night off, I had the night off. I was a starter for the most part, so chances were high that regardless of what happened to the other goalie,

I wasn't going in that night. Once I made the jump to the pro level, I learned that you could be thrown in at any given moment. It didn't matter if somebody got sick, got hurt, or was just having a tough game; suddenly you're getting thrown in there. I wasn't properly prepared for that right away. A lot of that had to do with maturity, and for myself, I've always been a late-bloomer. Things have always just come a little bit later to me compared to most other guys."

Goldman: Which proves how important it is to trust the process, even when all you want to do is keep pushing forward.

McElhinney: "That's not necessarily a bad thing, either. Everybody's different. But I think for me, it was just getting ready to play whether I was starting a game or not. That was the biggest challenge and the hardest thing to learn, especially once I made that jump to the NHL with Calgary. I was playing behind [Miikka] Kiprusoff at the time, and I think he had played 76 out of 82 games for almost four years in a row, which is just ridiculous for a starting goalie. But he was just so durable and the team was so reliant upon him that it worked. But to go every six-to-eight weeks without playing and then get thrown in there was certainly a very challenging thing to learn and manage. But long term, it was a good thing. I'm not necessarily saying I wanted to start out as a full-time backup, but it worked out in the end. You get pegged into that role after your first couple of years, depending on how the team views you or where they see you fitting in, and I have been stuck in it ever since."

Goldman: This is a story we hear pretty often with a lot of guys. A top college goalie struggles for a little while when he's used sparingly to begin his pro career.

McElhinney: "I think it was tough to embrace that grind at first. You have aspirations of being a starting goalie and playing a lot of games, because that's what you've done your entire career. Then when you make that jump to the next level, maybe you don't necessarily have the talent level from the team's perspective to carry them for 65 games, so you get pigeonholed into that role, and then you learn how to become a backup goalie in the NHL. It was tough. It was probably one of the hardest things I ever had to do. It's been a good challenge throughout my career, and now that I look back on it, I try to embrace it a little bit more. It still took until l was 26 or 27 before I fully embraced that challenge."

Goldman: Because of where you were drafted and what most scouts perceived you to be, how hard was it to stay patient when you were trying to prove to NHL teams that you can fill a role behind a guy like Kiprusoff? They're always looking for experienced guys, but you're not getting the games you need to prove you have the necessary experience.

McElhinney: "It was by far the hardest thing I ever had to do. I was up and down for about two years before I got traded to Anaheim, and that was almost a relief in a sense, because I was going into a new situation. Obviously they know what your history is, and it's not that I was going there to take over a job, but I was basically going to become a backup again. Still, I was hoping it would be a situation that would provide me with a few more games."

Goldman: Which it did. I remember how hard you battled your way into more starts in Anaheim.

McElhinney: "It honestly was such a relief to play some more games and get into a regular routine. I was back into the backup role again the next year, but was still playing more regularly. So I don't think I really embraced it in Calgary as much as in Anaheim. I resented the situation for the fact that they played Kipper so much. I felt like I could do the job, but I don't think I was fully embracing the opportunity to play, whether that happened every five days or once every two months. I wasn't mentally ready for that grind, and that was something that probably took me a few more years to fully comprehend, accept, and go, alright, if that's the situation, I need to be ready to go at a moment's notice. When I was 24, it certainly wasn't the case mentally for me, unfortunately."

Goldman: Was there ever a point during your time with Calgary where the thought, "Screw this, I'm done!" ever crossed your mind? Did thoughts of quitting ever weigh on you or keep you up at night?

McElhinney: "It's not that I didn't want to play anymore, but it was like I just got used to always sitting and never playing. Sometimes that's the most difficult part for a backup goalie, especially behind a guy that plays 70-plus games. Kipper and I have drastically different styles. We're totally opposite for the most part [laughing]. But you start watching a guy night-in, night-out and you almost start trying to play like him. You start picking up some of his habits, which isn't conducive whenever the team does need you to play well and win games. I can't go out there and try to play like Miikka Kiprusoff. It's just not going to correlate to success. That was the other hard part for me. It's something I didn't learn until I was around 26 or 27. I almost just stopped watching our goalie if I was backing up. By that time, I knew that I had a system developed for what gave me success on the ice and I wanted to stick to that. The moment you start watching a guy thinking you're going to play like him because he's having success is when you start getting into trouble. That's what happened to me in Calgary."

Goldman: So you went through this transformation pretty early in your pro career. It took a few years, but it sounds like you eventually discovered that you had to start embracing your own unique style.

McElhinney: "Yeah. When you're playing regularly, you don't really think about it, because you always know what's working. You're already in the rhythm of being on the ice, doing your thing in practice, and getting into games. For the most part, I had success up to that point. You're just trying to get the work that you need in practice so that you can perform in games. But in reality, I wasn't sticking to what made me successful in games while I was practicing. I was trying to do stuff that just wasn't my style of play. I think that's what really threw me off from the time I was 24 until I was 28. I just got lost. I didn't really know what my true identity was. The good thing was that I went back to the AHL, started playing more games, and got back into that rhythm where I could work everything out on the ice. When you're playing regularly, it's easier than trying to get those reps in practice."

Goldman: Being on five different NHL teams now, you've pushed through many reassignments and recalls. You've also worked with a bunch of goalie coaches. Going through this process of re-identifying what made you successful, what was it like trying to deal with all of the feedback and advice you were getting from different coaches? That happens with a lot of younger American goalies. They bounce around from team to team and have nearly 10 goalie coaches in just a few years. It's

not always easy to find yourself when everyone is telling you to be something slightly different.

McElhinney: "I think the epiphany came when I got to Columbus. By then, I knew what felt good when I was on the ice. I knew what I was doing right when I was having success. The difficult part was to put that into words with an actual system; something I could translate into a practice and show coaches that, when I did these certain things right, I would have success. I knew what the feeling was when I was on the ice. If I was balanced on my edges, I felt like I could do whatever I needed to get into position and make saves, challenge here, or give up a little bit of depth there. But I never put it into an actual system until I was with Columbus. I give lots of credit to Ian Clark for helping me put that system into words and develop something that I could fall back on. If I started straying away from it on the ice and I wasn't really feeling it anymore, I could always go back to the system that I had written out and fully understood. It was easier to grasp my game."

Goldman: Yeah, that's awesome to hear. That idea of having a game plan is something I've learned from Thomas Magnusson [Swedish Hockey Federation]. It's almost like you gathered all this information over the years, both internally and externally, and then that system all came together when you started working with Ian in Columbus.

McElhinney: "There were basic fundamentals to my game that would lead to success. Once I got back to those in practice and stuck to the system that I had developed, I would get that feeling back on the ice quicker and easier. Up to that point, I had always just relied on feeling. It's easier to rely on feel when you're playing regularly, because you can work the kinks out. If you're not playing on a regular basis, it's a lot tougher."

Goldman: What I've learned over the past few years working with NHL goalies is the importance of not only having a structured game plan, but writing it out. Diagramming it. Looking at lines on the ice and evolving your understanding of situations. It's all about what you do with your techniques and stances in different situations, and very few goalies – even some that are just breaking into pro hockey – don't necessarily have a

great understanding of their specific game plan. It sounds like you went through a similar process; you got to a certain point where you finally had a full comprehension of your actual game plan.

McElhinney: "It literally changed everything for me. For the most part, you're always just experimenting along the way. Whatever the situation was, you knew you had a basic system, but it was all based on feeling. When I got to Columbus, I was able to put it into words and it was much easier. All of the situations were laid out in front of me and I knew if I just stuck to those, the 'feel' would come with it, and it would translate to more success on the ice."

Goldman: What else have you learned from working with Ian the past three seasons? How has he helped you expand your knowledge and toolbox?

McElhinney: "It's been a great relationship. We've butted heads every now and then, but I think that's a good thing for both guys. I think the biggest thing for Ian is not necessarily something he taught me mentally, but it's just his work in helping me develop that system. The tough part of being a backup is when you stop 40 out of 42 shots and win a game 3-2. You're feeling good afterwards, but the reality is that the starting goalie is going right back in the next game. For the most part, it doesn't matter how well you play. Especially when you're in a situation where you're playing behind a true starter, you're not going to change that role. So I think the hardest part was learning how to take those next two weeks off after a strong game, jump back in there, and still feel the success you had from that previous win or strong game. But the biggest thing with Ian was always making sure I had that system in place, so if I had to take three or four weeks off, when I went back in there, I was going to have the same good feeling, because I had been hammering home that system in the practices between games. That has been the biggest asset to the mental side of my game, even though a lot of it is technical work on the ice. It gives me that confident feeling when I do finally get back in there."

Goldman: In terms of embracing the backup role, maybe it doesn't come with a lot of accolades or love every night, but you still play a vital role on the team. Knowing that you had embraced it by the time you got

to Columbus, is there still any aspect of it that you struggle with right now heading into the 2016-17 season?

McElhinney: "The major thing that happened to me was when I got traded from Anaheim. I basically went from a high to a low and got traded on the low. It all happened in the blink of an eye. That was the breaking point where I said, 'Alright, where is my career going right now? What is this leading to? Can I still play? Am I just going to grind it out a few more years in the minors and wrap this up?' I ended up signing with Phoenix the following year and was doing alright in their minor league system. Nothing special, just kind of puttering along, until next thing I know, I have this major, major injury. I needed surgery, and the doctors told me they had only seen this injury in really bad motorcycle and bull riding accidents."

Goldman: What?! Bull riding?!

McElhinney: "Yeah. I tore off both lower abdominals and fractured my pelvis. I'm not sure if it was cracked all the way through, but the doctors were talking about how to stabilize it in different ways. It was quite a bit of force I generated. I don't know how I pulled that off."

Goldman: And you did this to yourself in a game?!

McElhinney: "We were playing in Manchester at the time. It was just a routine face-off play and it happened right off the draw. The puck went D-to-D and the guy took a nasty one-timer. It was one of those shots where I stretched out for it, but by the way I was watching the puck miss the net, the force of the abdominals pulling off the bone and the pelvis cracking felt so strong that I was convinced the puck had somehow hit me right in the midsection. It was so painful."

Goldman: That's insane. I've never heard of a goalie ever having an injury quite like that.

McElhinney: "I remember having to get back on the bus and walk to my car after the game. I was on crutches and had to get in my car and drive. To this day, I do not remember how I was able to drive home by myself, because I was in Maine and there was snow and ice everywhere. So it was certainly a long and tough recovery. It was the first injury I sustained that really forced me to miss some time."

Goldman: Just hearing from the media that you tore an abdominal muscle doesn't give you a good understanding of how much that must have hurt. How much of a grind was that for you?

McElhinney: "That was a little unusual and not something I necessarily wanted to hear from the doctors, but I was just lying on the operating table and listening to them tell me that they don't know if I will be able to play again after this surgery. They said, 'We'll figure things out once we get in there and kind of determine whether or not you still have a chance to play. If not, you'll probably just be walking everywhere. There won't be any physical activity or running or any of that stuff.' I remember they talked about putting this big Kevlar belt buckle on my pelvis. That whole time I was going, 'Whoa, hold on a second. This is pretty scary stuff.' I thought I was fine even after I got injured, so I think all of that was my breaking point."

Goldman: How long were you on the shelf? It had to be all season, right?

McElhinney: "It took almost eight months to recover, and while I was injured I got traded to Columbus. They decided to sign me as a third guy to help out in the minors. It was just one of those summers where I was just dying to give it one more shot. All I wanted to do was get one more kick at the can and make it back to the NHL. Long story short, I ended up getting that break, Columbus had faith in me, and they signed me to be their backup the following year. I knew that if I was coming back I was going to only be a backup. I had to fully embrace that role this time and take it on as a challenge. I said alright, I might go six or eight weeks without playing a game again, so I better be just as good in April as I was in the preseason."

Goldman: That's a grind all by itself, just waiting to get healthy enough to get back on the ice and continue filling your role. Is that why the injury was your breaking point?

McElhinney: "It was so frustrating and the recovery was so slow that it felt like it was never going to happen. I think the blessing for me was that it happened during the lockout year. Our camp for Springfield, Columbus's farm team at the time, started on September 26, so I had a little bit of extra time to get there. After about a month of sitting on my couch and not being able to walk, I was pretty hell-bent on playing, and once I set my mind to something, you're not going to convince me otherwise. I still remember a conversation I had with my agent, just sitting there in Maine telling him that I wanted to stick this out in North America and that I wanted one more shot at getting back into the NHL. It was one of those blessings in disguise, because I was traded while I was injured. I am grateful to the Columbus organization for taking that initial chance on me. Going through the grind of recovering from that injury could have been career-ending, but they gave me a shot and it's worked out pretty well. I'm so grateful for that."

Goldman: I'm curious about this, because I feel it in my own career and I see it in other goalies. It's almost like the more you try and force things to happen, the less success you have. But when you're able to let go and trust the process, regardless of injuries or a lack of playing time, you actually have more success. It just sort of happens. Is that something you feel like you may have experienced in your career?

McElhinney: "Yeah, and I think the big thing about injuries, depending on where they are, is the timing of them. When you sustain one, it allows you to step back. If it happens at the beginning of the season and you know you're going to be back, sometimes you don't really pull yourself away from the game and think things through, because you're just hell-bent on getting back on the ice even though you may not have fully recovered. My injury was so severe that allowed me to truly step away from everything for quite a while. There was literally no involvement with hockey, I was just sitting on my couch for the remainder of the season. There was certainly a lot of time and ways to think about how to make myself better, or how to get myself back to that level, even if it was just for one more game. What can I do to help me to get back there? The mental side of it was something where I just convinced myself that I was going to get there. The fact that I ended up signing with Columbus's farm team, meeting Ian, and developing some new techniques in my game was a perfect storm for me. That was the biggest thing. I could've probably come back and played a game or two, but I wouldn't have been able to stick around for another three years at this level. I needed to get the technical side straightened out with Ian."

Goldman: So in a bit of an ironic twist, it was the biggest setback of your pro career that ultimately led to everything coming full circle for you. That defined your unique grind.

McElhinney: "Yeah, and I really love the challenge now. After dealing with the fallout from that injury, it's all gravy now. I really enjoy this, and I'm embracing it as much as possible. I love the fact I'm on a young team — there's a lot of energy here and it's fun to be around. Obviously the struggles of not winning is challenging, but I think the growth is coming. To know that I'm possibly helping to lay the foundation for goalies here to have success in the future, or to show them the way to have success in the future, is an exciting thing. That's the thing I'm starting to truly value. You still want to go out and have success and prove you're an asset to the team on the ice; that's always the primary objective. But there are a lot of ways and intangible stuff that you don't really see, all the behind-the-scenes stuff that kind of really adds value to this role for me."

Goldman: Speaking of "behind the scenes" stuff, I always try to teach goalies that it's not what you know, but *who* you know and how you treat people. Can you talk about that since you've been on five different clubs and backed up some big-name guys like Kiprusoff and Bobrovsky? How important is it to approach your role from a relationship standpoint?

McElhinney: "When you're used to playing all the time and being the guy, you realize that for the most part, everyone else who has made it to the NHL has been the guy for their entire career. Then you get to the highest level and realize that the hardest part is knowing there are some guys that are just exceptional. They deserve to be in that spot and you're always going to play second-fiddle to them. So you ask, 'How can I be an asset to a Sergei Bobrovsky? What can I do to make him better?' I look at him on the ice and there's not much I can tell him that will make him any better [laughing]. But there's got to be some way that I can help him. Maybe it's with the mental side, maybe it's being someone to talk to, or maybe it's just being a distraction from the game at times, too."

Goldman: I love what you're saying, because it points to an egoless approach. You bring some fun and balance to the daily grind, because it's

not about you, but the other guys. That alone makes you a great asset to any team looking for veteran support and depth.

McElhinney: "I think that's important, because a lot of times we get caught up and so involved with the game that we really need to get our mind off it. The biggest challenge for me right now in that role is just trying to be an asset. Not necessarily on the ice all the time for the team, but maybe it could be a coach, too. How can I help them make this team better? I think that's the biggest thing that organizations are looking for. If your starting goalie means I only play 10 to 25 games, well there's going to be a lot of down time in between. So how am I going to contribute to this team in a positive manner? When you're young and you expect to play, it can be a difficult role to accept. You certainly don't want to get stuck in that role. Everybody plans on being a starting goalie in the NHL, but it's not a reality for a lot of us. I think you have to realize that you're fortunate to have made it to this level and realize you're a part of something that is bigger than you."

Goldman: So let's say you're sitting at the dinner table, and across from you is Curtis McElhinney just a few days before his very first start in the AHL. What advice would you give your younger self?

McElhinney: "I think the biggest thing I would say to him is to not take yourself so seriously. A lot of times and in a lot of situations, we put way more pressure on ourselves than necessary. I think we interpret people's outside expectations and we place them on ourselves, whereas in reality, once the moment has passed, whether it be a day, a year, or five years, you look back on everything and realize that it wasn't a big deal. It wasn't really that important. At the end of the day, it's just a game, so I would tell my younger self to relax a little bit and enjoy the moment."

Goldman: That's a really good answer.

McElhinney: "It's a hard thing to do though. I think that's the difficult part [laughing]. It's easy for me to sit here and tell some kid to not take those expectations so seriously, or to not put so much pressure on yourself. But it's a different thing to do it when you're in that environment."

Goldman: But just having your message portrayed to kids is so important. I guarantee you that a bunch of young goalies will be reading this chapter before a huge game, and your words will help them! When you're in the moment, you're so caught up in all of those little things that you want, and it seems like that checklist gets longer and longer the older you get. It makes your advice that much more important. Whenever you can just take a single moment to look at the bigger picture, or even just breathe and step back for a minute and have some fun, you're going to benefit from it.

McElhinney: "I don't remember when I got my first AHL start in Omaha, but I do remember that one of my first games was backing up Brent Krahn. This was a maturity thing, but my primary concern was the fact that I didn't have to wear a helmet on the bench anymore. So all I cared about was looking good on the bench, whether it was going with a hat or fixing my hair to make sure I was on that night [laughing]. Well, we absolutely got smoked, and I ended up getting thrown in. But I was so concerned with looking good, I forgot my helmet in the dressing room, so everyone had to wait on me to go in there, get my helmet, and get back out on the ice. It took about two minutes to get back down the tunnel, but it felt like an eternity. I went into the game, stopped one shot, and then our coach put Krahn right back in. He pulled me to the side and continued to educate me on what it meant to be a professional hockey player. That experience helped teach me how to be prepared on a nightly basis. So there are certainly some enjoyable moments that I look back on, but they weren't enjoyable at the time [laughing]."

Goldman: Maybe that's what "Embracing the Grind" is all about for a backup goalie in the NHL. Just being at peace with all of the things that you can't control, but also what you have controlled and what you have done, right? Even when you do the wrong things.

McElhinney: "I can look back on my career and honestly say that I wouldn't change a single negative thing that has happened to me. I might do it a little differently if I got the opportunity, and obviously I've been pretty fortunate through all the ups and downs, but I don't regret any of it. I guess you could say I'm at peace with it all."

Chapter 6
LEARN HOW TO WORK

"You can't get much done in life if you only work on the days when you feel good." - Jerry West

When given a chance to reflect on their careers, one of the most common regrets we hear from NHL goalies is how they wish they worked a bit differently. Some of them wanted to work harder. Some wanted to work smarter. Some wanted to work with more of a purpose. Others expressed their regret for not working more consistently during the early days of their career.

Whatever the regret, there's one thing all goalies learn: Hard work isn't easy. *Learning* how to work, however, could be even tougher to accomplish. In fact, it's a subject scientists still study at the neurological and sociological levels with a fevered pitch.

Is work ethic a predisposed genetic trait? Is it something coded deep in your DNA? Is there a way to tweak or alter that code as you mature? Is it tied to your unique environment and culture? Do farmers have better odds of developing a stronger work ethic than city dwellers? What elements directly influence one's work habits? Is it an endless debate of nature versus nurture?

Although the science behind the inner-workings of one's work ethic continues to be a polarizing subject, there are three things every goalie and goalie coach can agree with: You can't coast through the process, you can't get by on skill alone, and you simply can't cheat the game.

We've all heard these three phrases before, but the lessons they teach must be repeated often, because they can take a lifetime to learn. They are simple morsels of truth that we all strive to live and play by. We all have the ability to look back and find instances where we could have worked harder, and we all learn through our experiences what it takes to work to the best of our abilities.

One way you can learn how to work better as a goaltender is by openly evaluating your efforts in practices and games. Have your goalie coach write down an honest evaluation of how hard you worked in different areas of the game, then have he or she write it down as a percentage. These areas could be categories like skating, tracking, team drills, warmups, or even your work ethic in the weight room. Does he or she think you worked to 80-percent of your ability? Fifty percent?

Now take a few minutes to write down your own percentages for the same categories. How hard do you feel you really worked? And be honest, otherwise you're just cheating yourself! When you're done, take 10 minutes to compare the percentages with your goalie coach and discuss what you can do to boost that percentage by five, 10, or 15 points over the next few weeks.

No matter what you do to learn how to work more effectively, the lesson here is that you have complete control in your work ethic. You can't control a lot of your predisposed genetics or much of your upbringing, but you can control your attitude.

No matter how many times you try and get away with a lazy effort, you can't cut corners in the circle of life, for a circle has no edges. Everything you do has some type of effect on your future. Good or bad, there is no action without consequence. Your ability to work harder and smarter is what keeps your wheel of fortune turning; it brings new beginnings and opens new doors.

Learning to work comes down to one thing — your willingness to realize that you can be better. To be blessed with a talent like goaltending takes its pain and sacrifice, and to reach where you are destined takes most of your life. With blood and sweat you soak your intentions, with pride and honor you set your sails, and with a more consistent effort, your attitude and your willingness to work harder will allow you to embrace the grind and ultimately prevail.

Chapter 7
JIMMY HOWARD

Introduction: *If we had to summarize his story in just one phrase, "Trust the process" would be our narrative of choice for one James Russell Howard III. After spending three years setting school and NCAA records with the University of Maine, the native of Ogdensburg, New York transitioned to the pro ranks and spent the next four years slowly honing his skills in the AHL. Finally, at the ripe age of 26, Howard would claim his starter's throne. For the next six years, he was known across the lands as the durable and gritty All-Star goaltender for the historic Detroit Red Wings. Despite carrying the workload for so long, everything changed when the young and electric Peter Mrazek started dazzling scouts and fans with his aggressive, dynamic style of play. Suddenly, Howard was forced to witness much of the 2015-16 season from the bench. Clearly struggling with the shift in roles and despite having suffered from the fallout of losing his starting gig, when Mrazek burned out and struggled late in the team's fierce playoff pursuit, Howard embraced the home stretch and was there when his team needed him the most, solidifying Detroit's return to the Stanley Cup Playoffs for an NHL-best 25 consecutive years.*

Valley: Let's say you're having dinner, and sitting across from you at the table is Jimmy Howard on the night before he's heading to the University of Maine for his freshman year. What advice would you give him about the journey he'll be taking over the next decade?

Howard: "I would tell him he should've started working a lot harder four or five years earlier [laughing]. I mean, I'd want him to know that he has to be ready, because it all starts here. You've got a short window of opportunity to make it and to sell yourself, so you have to be ready to get it done."

Valley: What would you tell him about all the emotional ups and downs?

Howard: "I would tell him it's a business. Believe it or not, even though it's just a game and it's supposed to be fun, at the end of the day, the NHL is a multi-million dollar industry, and it's a great one at that. Unfortunately, there's an expiration date on playing in it, too. So you just have to be ready."

Valley: Did you feel like you were ready when you finished college and started your pro career?

Howard: "I'll be honest with you. I wasn't ready. I didn't realize what it would take. To me, I was just playing hockey, and then all of a sudden it was like, wow, I'm in the NHL. It was a dream come true, especially being a small kid from Ogdensburg, New York. But I just wasn't ready for an 82-game schedule at all, so it was an absolute grind for me. It took me three years [in the AHL] just to figure out how to get through a season without suffering from exhaustion."

Valley: During those three years, did you feel like it was more of a physical or a mental grind?

Howard: "I would say it was more mental. By the time February rolled around, I was just exhausted from riding the bus from town to town. Sometimes you're not getting in until 5:00 in the morning, and then you're expected to go out that night and perform."

Valley: With no excuses, whatsoever.

Howard: "None at all. And that was my biggest fear. But eventually I figured out how to train like a pro and handle the fact that it's a non-stop lifestyle. You take your two weeks off at the end of the season, but then you have to get your ass right back in there, because like it or not, somebody else wants your job, no matter what position you're playing."

Valley: You said that it took you a couple of years to learn that lesson. Do you remember if someone ever took you aside and gave you that pep

talk, or did you figure it out on your own? When was your breakthrough point?

Howard: "Of course I had guys early on in my career that would sit down and talk to me and help me out. Ozzie [Chris Osgood], Kris Draper, Cheli [Chris Chelios], Malts [Kirk Maltby], the list goes on and on. Fortunately, I was in a situation where Detroit could develop me slowly and let me figure out everything on my own. It was my third season in the American Hockey League when I finally figured it out. That was the year I was an AHL All-Star and everything just started clicking for me. Not that my rookie season was a bad one; I was runner-up for Rookie of the Year and named to the All-Rookie team. But I'll be honest. That year in February and then when the playoffs began, I was done. I was exhausted."

Valley: So when we say it's more emotional than physical, part of that is handling the expectations of being great every night. How do you get that across to people? Do you have to go through it to truly know how to handle it?

Howard: "Now don't get me wrong, I love the fact that I went to college. It was always my dream to play in the NCAA. Growing up, that's the only thing I knew. Being close to both St. Lawrence and Clarkson, I would always go to those games with my dad, so I think I've always wanted to play college hockey. But for the guys that *do* play major-juniors, I think they can come in really prepared for the change to the pro game, because they're already playing a 60-plus game schedule and riding the bus every day. So I think they already have a clue about what they will be going through, whereas I think many college guys have to go through it before they can really understand it."

Valley: So did you feel ready when you first broke into the NHL?

Howard: "In my mind, I thought I was, until I actually got on the ice for my first preseason game and realized that, wow, this is a major step. It wasn't a little one at all. Going from the USNTDP [National Team Development Program] to the University of Maine, well, I was already prepared for that, thanks to the NTDP's schedule, which is modeled like a college schedule. Once I got into an NHL preseason game, for the first few [games], it felt like it was so fast and everyone were so good. And these guys weren't even going hard."

Valley: I always looked at you as a mentally tough guy. I don't know if it's the swagger you had, or maybe it's something that resonated in me during a few big games around the playoffs. Do you feel like you're a mentally tough goalie?

Howard: "I feel like a mentally tough goaltender. I feel like I've been through a lot and I've always seemed to come out of it stronger. At the same time, I also believe that I'm more of a workhorse. I'm a guy that will go in there night-in, night-out and just play. I think when you're doing that, everything else goes by the wayside. You're not thinking, you're just playing. It wasn't until last season when I was just sitting there, thinking way too much, that stuff started to falter."

Valley: You said earlier you went through a lot of situations that made you mentally tougher. Obviously, we have to go through the ups and downs; we're not born with mental toughness. What are some of the tougher lows you've had to battle through?

Howard: "The toughest one in my professional career was this past season [2015-16]. I was relegated to the backup position and had no clue when I was going to start my next game. It could've been once every 10 or 12 days, or on the tail end of a back-to-back. Either way, I struggled to go out there and perform. Figuring out how to handle that situation has been the toughest part of my pro career."

Valley: What kind of emotional challenges did you face during that time? What happens to you mentally when that type of major role change takes place?

Howard: "You start over-analyzing your play. You start over-thinking it and then you start forcing things. Instead of letting the puck hit you, you're trying to make saves, because you want to get in there and make yourself feel better, instead of just letting the thing hit you. That's when I'm playing my best; I'm just letting the puck hit me and just competing."

Valley: The Jimmy Howard that I would watch when we came into Detroit was a guy that was mentally tough and a guy that could compete and come up with the big saves at the right time. How did you embrace that whole situation?

Howard: "I maintained a positive frame of mind to the best of my ability. I tried to be happy and show up to the rink ready to work with a smile on my face every single day. I just worked like a dog [laughing]. Jim Bedard was out there, and I was one of the first guys on the ice and one of the last guys off. I worked out and continued to stay in the weight room. Basically just got after it, I guess. I had to reboot my entire system and learn how to mentally prepare for only playing once in a while."

Valley: Was there anybody outside of the rink that was supporting you, or did you keep most of this internal?

Howard: "My family and my wife were huge through this whole situation. Another guy who has always been in my corner is Chris Osgood. He was really beneficial for me during this time. Pretty much all of my family and friends were very helpful with the whole thing. They kept me upbeat, focused, and on track. They just kept telling me that eventually I'll come out of this, and I did."

Valley: That was at the end of the season, when you had to rally and find your confidence. Petr Mrazek hit the wall, and you were able to get the points the Red Wings needed to make the playoffs. That's a pretty amazing thing, because it would have been so easy to just not be ready for the call. But all of a sudden, you were there, and that just shows how hard you worked to put yourself in a position to be ready when the chance came.

Howard: "We competed the best we could in the playoffs, but we ran into a better team. Tampa Bay was just better than us for four out of the five games that we played."

Valley: With the challenges you faced when that happened, or maybe in other tough stretches, what would you have done differently to get through it?

Howard: "I would've relaxed more. I think I got myself too wound up and felt like I had to go out there and be the 1st Star every single time I played. I thought that was the only way I was going to have a chance at getting my starting job back. Like I said earlier, that backfired, because then I was just forcing myself to make saves."

Valley: It's so hard to tell any goalie that the answer is to just relax more, but that's truly the answer. You almost have to completely take yourself out of the situation and realize that this isn't the be-all, end-all. You are talented, so as soon as the situation allows, you'll be able to show that. But telling a goalie to just relax is tough. It's your livelihood and you're programmed to be the guy winning games. All of a sudden when you're not doing it, you realize just how tough it is to relax. Hannu [Nykvist] gave me an analogy once. He said, "If you're going fishing, be prepared to wait."

Howard: "It's so true, you have to be patient. By the way, I hate fishing [laughing]."

Valley: So we've talked about your toughest times, but if you look back, what would you say was *the* best point of your NHL career? When did you have the most fun playing?

Howard: "My rookie season was unbelievable. I had so much fun playing out there every night. It was a new test every single game. It was just so much fun just to be out there on the ice with so many great hockey players on the team."

Valley: Were you ever nervous at all?

Howard: "The only time I was ever nervous was in my first game with the Red Wings. I wasn't nervous at all leading up to it. Then one of our captains came up to me right before I hit the ice for my first NHL start in Los Angeles and said,

'Congratulations, kid. I know it's going to be the first of many. But you better not *f****ing* [expletive] lose tonight.' Of course right away I got butterflies [laughing]. But I went on the ice and started playing and all the nerves just went away. We ended up winning the game, 5-2."

Valley: A lot of NHL goalies say that when things are going great, you're not thinking. You're just playing, smiling, making memories. It's not an emotional grind to go to the rink, because you're having fun. All of a sudden, when you do go through a struggle, now it becomes a business, and now you're over-thinking, you're tired, and then it becomes emotionally draining.

Howard: "Well, that was the biggest thing. I needed to relax more. I'd be so high-strung all the time trying to figure out what I was doing wrong or what I could be doing better. I'd have hockey on every single night, watching other goalies play throughout the league, trying to pick up little tidbits here and there. When things are going well, I might not even watch hockey. If I do, it's usually so that my wife and I can just enjoy a game together and not really think about it."

Valley: When I hear that, I'd say you were looking for answers where there were none to be found. The answers are inside you already. You're a world-class goalie, just relax, smile, and go have fun.

Howard: "Exactly. But nobody was telling me that per se. At the same time, I didn't really show those emotions around anybody, either."

Valley: There's a sense of pride there, too. You've been the guy there for so long. But it's funny, once you learn that lesson, you look back and you're almost like, what was I doing?

Howard: "Why was I beating not only myself up, but stressing my wife out? She didn't want to see me going through this. I needed to just relax. Once I relaxed, and I think that happened in Denver for the Outdoor Game, I finally figured it out. When I got the start in the next game in Dallas, I played really well, we won, and then it just kept snowballing."

Valley: Did you ever reach a point where you just said, "You know what? I don't really care anymore. Whatever happens, happens. I'm just going to be myself."

Howard: "I think that's a fair assessment, but I don't think it's a static way of thinking. You still care and still want to win. It's more like you finally take a deep breath and let the weight of the whole world slide off your shoulders. That's basically how it felt."

Valley: When I was younger, we didn't really have goalie coaches or people we could talk to about these things. We had to figure it out ourselves.

Howard: "Same here. When I first came into the AHL in 2005, I had a goalie coach [Jim Bedard]. But I never really got a chance to see him, because he was always in Detroit working with Ozzie and Manny [Legace] and Dom [Dominik Hasek], and rightfully so, because that's the big club. So I don't think people understand that I had to figure a lot out by myself. A lot was just conversing with my dad, because he coached me a lot growing up. Or I'd talk to old goalie coaches that I knew, specifically Grant Standbrook and Barry Madigan. But a lot of it I had to figure out on my own, and I think that's what made me more mentally tough."

Valley: I see a lot of younger goalies really struggle to develop that mental toughness, because they have a goalie coach by their side their entire lives.

Howard: "Thank you for seeing that in me, but at the same time, I've been that way my whole life. It didn't matter if I was playing street hockey on the road or a huge game in college, I was going to win. There were no ifs, ands, or buts about it — I was going to win. That's the way I've always been and I'm still programmed to be that way today. Even when I go play golf with my buddies, it pisses me off to no end when I have to hand them over cash. I will go out there and just absolutely grind it out to win."

Valley: You can't teach that. You either have it or you don't, and you have it, which again is one of the things that makes you really good.

Howard: "Well, I'm fortunate it was passed on by the Howard gene."

Valley: Who are some of the most influential people that you've had in your life?

Howard: "My grandfather, Jim Howard I, and my dad, Jim Howard II. Barry Madigan, the goalie coach out of Ottawa, and then I'd say Darren Mabley. Darren pretty much taught me my swag. When I first showed up in Ann Arbor, he was like, 'You've got no swag. You've got to carry yourself better. You're this shy, quiet, little guy — go find some mojo.' He really worked on that with me. Then I'd have to say Grant Standbrook at the University of Maine. Absolute living legend. I've never learned so much about hockey than from him. Then Jim Bedard obviously, for sticking with me for 11 years."

Valley: Let me ask you about your dad and grandfather. What are some of the best lessons you learned from them?

Howard: "Well my dad always told me that you're only as good as your last outing. It doesn't matter if you played well or you're good, if you played like crap in your last game, you're crap. That's what he always taught me, and he tried to instill and build that consistency in me. Is it going to happen every single night? No. We all know that. You don't have to be great every night, but be good, and that's what I try to do. My grandfather also taught me a lot. He's actually in the national Wrestling Hall of Fame, so he was a coach for a really long time at Oswego State and taught me a lot of life lessons. When he'd take me golfing or fly fishing, he'd just talk and tell me about things and teach me how you go out there and get things done."

Valley: Is Jimmy Howard a better goalie today than he was 365 days ago?

Howard: "I am. I think what I went through last season has prolonged my career, because now I know how to do both. If I end up not playing every 10-to-11 days this year, I'm going to be relaxed. I'm just going to go out there every day and get prepared for when I am starting."

Chapter 8
Be a Student of Life

"Failure is only the opportunity to begin again, this time more intelligently." - Henry Ford

The wise goaltender eventually learns that there are as many techniques as there are situations. The wise goalie coach eventually learns that there are as many styles as there are goalies. The wise individual eventually learns that the learning process actually has no end.

The grinds you face in life are exactly the same — they never truly end. They are extensions of your past and forever tied to your future. Today is the tomorrow you were promised yesterday; all of your choices will manifest new problems, solutions, paths, and learning experiences. For this reason alone, goalies must be students of the game and life in general. Success in both realms rarely comes to the close-minded or the know-it-all.

Always be willing to learn from others, even if you don't necessarily agree with them or appreciate their merits. Learn from those not only above you, but below you as well. Strive to place zero judgement on the voice or the message — don't just hear what others say, truly listen.

Furthermore, always be willing to learn new things, even if they're on topics or subjects you dislike. You may hate math, but goaltending is intimately tied to geometry. The more you study it, the better goalie you will be, both consciously and unconsciously. A creative mind is able to make connections, weak or strong, between any of the infinite realms of universal knowledge and goaltending. Martial arts, meditation, yoga, and other disciplines that seem totally unrelated to stopping pucks can offer a vast cornucopia of key skills that will make you a better goalie.

Goaltending is an art, a science, a form of dance, and when done properly, music to our ears. The goalies that are willing to learn about these varying topics are always expanding their knowledge base and therefore always getting better.

As a goalie, being a student calls for a special type of openness. You need to be able to accept the fact that you don't have all the answers. In a game where you're forced to be an emotional rock and the backbone of a team, it's not always easy to reach down and admit that you may be doing the wrong things or making mistakes. So you need to be in tune with yourself. You can never be afraid to admit you have weaknesses.

You must also be willing to allow others to give honest and sometimes harsh criticism without judging or ignoring them. You can't resist those who are trying to help you by giving honest feedback. Without it, you're trapped in a shell of unknowing. You don't always have to agree with or use the advice you get, but at least be willing to listen and accept what others say.

As you will come to learn, there's an everlasting archetype embedded deep in the goalie's code. It states, *"The older I get, the more experience I gain, the more I know."* This is certainly true to an extent, but if you want to be a student of life, shift your way of thinking and imagine the world this way:

"The older I get, the more experience I gain, the more I learn."

Chapter 9
Jordan Sigalet

Introduction: *No book on the goaltender's grind would be complete without hearing from Calgary Flames goalie coach Jordan Sigalet. The story behind his Multiple Sclerosis diagnosis during his time at Bowling Green University is downright scary, because nothing can prepare you at that age for being hit with that type of life-altering news. But his story weaves a beautiful tapestry of perseverance and sacrifice, making him a great mentor and a key icon in the world of goaltending. Fortunately, upon sharing the news with the world, Jordan received the support he needed from friends, family, and the Boston Bruins franchise to push on. He played for as long as he could, and then went straight into coaching. Onward he fights, dealing with the physical and emotional hurdles that come with managing MS. On top of this, he makes no excuses when it comes to his coaching duties with the Flames. He still spends the endless hours cutting video, the early mornings scouting opposing goalies, and everything that goes into preparing for the NHL draft. This puts everything into an important perspective, especially when he's working directly with his students. No matter what they're going through, Jordan simply has to tell them that things could be a whole lot worse. This not only makes him an ideal role model for goalies at the professional level, but it makes him an ideal friend as well. And at the end of the day, when your career comes to an end and the skates are hung up for good, friends and memories are all you have left.*

Goldman: You've been through plenty of adversity in your personal life and playing career. So when I tell you about the theme of this book, what do you first reflect upon?

Sigalet: "There's so many ups and downs in the game of hockey, but the biggest grind for me was my college experience. Before I was diagnosed with Multiple

Sclerosis, I came out of junior hockey in Victoria as the go-to guy for the Salsa, so I was playing every single game. When I got to Bowling Green University, I expected to just keep playing every game again, but it turned out to be a huge eye-opener for me. I got there as a freshman behind a very good goalie named Tyler Masters and hardly even played my entire first year. Emotionally, that was really tough. I let myself go mentally and physically, I got a bit overweight as a freshman, and just got depressed from not playing. I had to embrace that, so I got a different attitude when I went home that summer. Before my sophomore year began, I lost 30 pounds and got in really good shape and went back with a totally different attitude. I was a changed person both mentally and physically, which allowed me to play almost half of the games that year. That really prepared me for the last two years, where I played in almost every game. Mentally, that was the biggest challenge I faced right away in my playing career."

Goldman: Until you received the scariest news of your life...

Sigalet: "The diagnosis happened in 2004 during my junior year at Bowling Green. I was playing one weekend up there against Northern Michigan and I woke up Saturday morning with a numb right foot. Some people wake up with pins and needles in their foot or their arm and that's just from sleeping on it funny, so that was my initial thought. But throughout the day that numbness never went away. Every time I took a step, it just kind of hummed and buzzed. I went to bed that night and just forgot about it, thinking it would be gone in the morning, but I woke up the next morning completely numb and weak from the chest down. It was so tingly that it almost felt like my whole body was asleep."

Goldman: Did you start to panic?

Sigalet: "At that point I got really worried, so I called the team doctor. He told me to come in, I did, and they ran some tests. I remember on the way to the hospital, the numbness started to get even stronger and spread into my face and neck. When I got to the hospital, they did a spinal tap, an MRI, and a bunch of neurological tests. Not long after that, the doctor came back in, and I remember him putting his hand on my leg and looking me in the eye and saying, 'Jordan, things don't look good.' I thought the next words out of his mouth were going to be cancer or a tumor, but he said, 'It looks like Multiple Sclerosis.' To hear those words — obviously I didn't know what the disease was or what it was going to do to me — was shocking. I thought the worst right away. My first question was, 'Is this going to kill me? Am I going to die?' My biggest questions at the time were whether or not I could still play. Hockey was my life, and I thought for sure that meant the end of hockey for me."

Goldman: Clearly there's no way to know you were going to get blindsided by something so shocking and traumatic. Was there a point when you first didn't accept the diagnosis?

Sigalet: "For sure. I mean, you're young and in the prime of your life. As a college athlete you feel invincible, so I was definitely in denial and didn't accept it. I actually got two or three more opinions, and that was the worst thing I did; it was like being diagnosed over and over again. But in my mind, I just wanted to be clear of what it was. Once I did accept it, I realized how I was going to treat that disease and live a normal life. After I was diagnosed, the worst thing was that I kept it to myself and kept it from my family for about six months. I didn't tell anyone. I was being drafted at the time by Boston, and I thought that if they found out I had MS, they'd sweep me under the rug and refuse to sign me to a pro contract. I had this fear and burden on my shoulders, and I just sat on it for a few months. Finally, I got sick of hiding behind the lies and excuses, because any time I wasn't feeling good, I had to make something up. I finally went public and it was a big weight off my shoulders. It gave me a chance to network with people who had the same disease. It gave me a chance to share my story and help others. On top of that, Boston was one of my biggest supporters. The support I received from around the hockey world was unbelievable, so I wish I would have gone public with it sooner."

Goldman: Knowing that goalies are bred to have a thick skin and knowing that keeping your diagnosis to yourself was a mistake, how important is it for goalies to open up?

Sigalet: "Going through all of that and still going through things on a daily basis has made me so much stronger mentally. It prepared me for this grind as a goalie coach in all of the NHL's high-pressure situations. I think that my goalies look at what happened to me and there's a respect level for what I've gone through, and what I have to go through on a daily basis. It definitely brings a bond between my goalies and I. It's special to have that; it helps earn the trust between the goaltenders. I think just hockey alone — growing up and playing a team sport that has so much adversity — helped prepare me for that diagnosis and how to handle it. Having teammates around and having the support of a whole team on top of your family makes a big difference."

Goldman: I have an older sister with MS, which is why I asked Mike if I could be the one to interview you. She's in her 50's now, but I've seen first-hand how she has good days and bad days. Emotionally, that must take a huge toll. In your case, not only are you managing MS, but you're logging a ton of hours cutting video, keeping your own personal goalie stats for the Flames, and traveling with the team. That workload alone is a tough grind for NHL goalie coaches, so how do you keep yourself going every day?

Sigalet: "It always sounds cliché when you say you have to live one day at a time, but it's true with this disease. I don't know what tomorrow's going to bring, so I find it's mentally exhausting and much harder when you're thinking about weeks, months, or years down the road. You don't know how it's going to be. You don't know what's going to happen. It's an unknown. So every time you wake up and have a good day, you appreciate it. Every day I step on the ice as an NHL goalie coach, I appreciate it more and more. Going through what I've gone through, coaching in the NHL gives me a good reason to wake up every morning and be happy. I love the job, but you just have to manage your sleep, your rest, and eating habits as good as you can, because sometimes it's hard to do on the road. You don't have much time to sleep, you have to get the rest when you can. When you do have bad days, you get through them with your medication and the support of your coaching staff, teammates and friends. I have to add three injections a week into my life, so I'm also managing those symptoms and potential side effects. It's easier now than when I was playing, because I think the pressure you feel mentally comes more from coaching. The physical exertion isn't there like I had when I was playing with the disease for five years. Heat is one of the biggest onsets of MS symptoms, so it was tough to manage that when I was playing. At least now it's just mostly the mental side that I have to manage these days."

Goldman: The past two seasons with Calgary have been a little bit of an up and down. What has it been like to work with a Swiss phenom and two Finnish goalies, all three of which were in very different stages of their careers?

Sigalet: "It's been fun to have three different styles to work with. Obviously Hiller comes from the Francois Allaire era, where he's a very calm and controlled blocking-style goalie in the net. Then you have Karri Ramo, who is definitely a lot more aggressive and athletic. And then Joni [Ortio] is up-and-coming and is a little bit of both of them. He's not as aggressive as Karri, but he's positionally sound and a bit on the smaller side in today's NHL. To work with all three personalities is great, because they're all receptive guys, but definitely in different stages of their careers. This year compared to last has obviously been a little up and down and a bit of a roller coaster. We had big expectations after last year, but we didn't meet those expectations this year, so mentally that's hard as a goalie coach, especially when you don't see your guys having success. Starting the year with three goalies was mentally hard on all of us. So it was definitely a tougher situation this year, but you just have to try and find that even keel and not get too high or too low, just like when you're playing. I realized that and just tried to go out there every day and make those guys better."

Goldman: I know so many things happen over the course of the season and every goalie gets rattled in different ways. Sometimes they're big things, but other times they're just little things that happen to get under their skin. Due to your battle with MS, you clearly have a very different perspective of the little things versus the big things. So when a guy gets rattled by something minor, how do you handle that situation?

Sigalet: "For sure. Guys go through things like that all the time and I've had conversations about how things could be a lot worse with my goalies. They could be out with injuries or go through something career-ending. So I talk about myself, I talk about Josh Harding, and I talk about how some people get hit with something sudden and it's career-ending and disabling. I think it just puts everything into perspective when you have to deal with something like that."

Goldman: I have the same kind of question for a guy who simply isn't working as hard as you know he can. How do you approach a goalie that is deceiving himself or taking shortcuts? How do you get him to grind it out a bit more?

Sigalet: "For me, it's all about building that good relationship where your goalies can trust you. It allows you to be stern with them and challenge them when needed. We had a goalie that came up at the start of the year, but he had a sense of entitlement. If he got hit in the head at practice, he was acting like a 10-year veteran. I had to sit him down and have a long talk with him and just say it how it is. It was almost like a father-son conversation, and when you have that relationship and that trust, I find it easy to do. They don't get mad at you and they listen, because it's coming from someone that they respect. When he came back here a second time, he was a different goaltender. He improved his work ethic in practice, he was the first one on the ice, and his battle level had totally changed. It was nice to see. But in my mind, you definitely have to be able to earn that trust before you can do something like that."

Goldman: This question is different from most, but it's one we're asking each guy in the book. What would you tell your younger self if he were sitting across from you at a dinner table right now? What would you tell him about the grind he's about to go through in college and as a goalie coach?

Sigalet: "I wish I knew what I know now when I was 16, just from seeing it from the other side of the business, seeing all the stuff behind the scenes. But I always had the mindset when I was playing that I was always going to be the hardest worker, that I was going to do more than everyone else out there, and just not give up on my dream. I think a lot of guys can't handle the ups and downs, but it was something that I was good at handling. I got cut from so many teams when I was an Atom, Peewee, and Bantam. Instead of being disappointed and packing it in, it just made me stronger. It made me want to work even harder and be even better. I think that's why I did get to play that short time in the NHL and backup with a few teams, and even though it was a short career, play as long as I did. I think I'd tell myself that there's going to be a lot of ups and downs and you just have to stick through it and stick to the process and be the hardest worker. Those things also sound cliché, but it's so true."

Goldman: Right now it's the summer and you're already starting to look forward to next season with your goaltenders. What kind of things are you doing over the summer to get better? Or are you a pretty hands-off guy in the off-season?

Sigalet: "I just try to keep learning more, gather more information, and talk to a lot of other NHL goalie coaches. A big influence in my coaching career has been Wade Flaherty with Winnipeg. When I was coaching for my first year in the WHL with Everett, they had Kent Simpson there. He was a Chicago [Blackhawks] draft pick and Wade was Chicago's development guy at the time. Wade lived in Langley, British Columbia and I lived just across the border in Washington. So every few weeks he'd come down and work with Kent, and I'd go down with him just to pick the guy's brain. He's been a huge influence of me for sure. I talk to guys like Mitch Korn all the time and you develop friendships and relationships with other goalie coaches and bounce ideas off each other. Going to the [NetWork Goaltending] symposium last year was a great learning experience, and obviously I'm going to do it again this summer. So it's just finding ways to get better and not being stubborn by thinking you know everything. You can learn from a Peewee goalie coach if you are open-minded and you're willing to learn from other people."

Goldman: Let's say I'm one of your students and I just got off the ice after a really bad game. Maybe I did all of the things I was supposed to do leading up to the game. I prepared, I didn't go out the night before with the guys, I stretched properly. I did all those things, but the puck dropped and everything fell apart. I crumbled out there and came off the ice pissed off, mad at the world, and didn't want to talk to anyone. What would you say to me if you were my coach? How would you handle that?

Sigalet: "I dealt with that almost every game this year [laughing]. For me sometimes, it's best to just let the goalie be. At this level, I'll usually give him his space until I know he's ready to talk. If it's one of my guys and he had a shitty game the previous night, I'm not showing him stuff from that shitty game, I'm showing him a highlight reel of saves from the two or three games before that just to build that confidence back up. Obviously bad games are going to happen, so it's not dwelling on the negative stuff, it's pulling out the positive stuff and talking about the things that he did well. Otherwise it's just a snowball effect out there."

Goldman: I wanted to wrap things up by asking you to reflect on something. We've asked every guy to define the grind, and it's fascinating how they all say the same thing. "It may seem like a grind and it is hard, but it's really not, because we love the game so much." The big teaching point is that, whether you're a banker, a bridge builder, or a brain surgeon, nothing will break you if you truly love it.

Sigalet: "I totally agree, from a playing and coaching perspective. I wake up every day and can't wait to go to the rink, whether it's after a win or a loss. You're going in there and getting to work with professional athletes and you get to spend half of your time working on the ice. It's where I love to be. It takes my mind off everything. Even when I got diagnosed, I just wanted to get back on the ice, because it took my mind away from all the negatives. It was my comfort zone and it still is today. When the season ends, you don't know what to do with yourself, because you're just itching to get back out there. It's tough watching the Stanley Cup Playoffs and the World Championships, because you're still surrounding yourself with a lot of hockey, but you're not playing in it. For sure it's a grind in the middle of a season; you're playing a lot of games, spending a lot of time together, and traveling a lot. But it's awesome, I love it, and I wouldn't want to be doing anything else in the world. It's a dream job. It wouldn't be fun if it *wasn't* a grind, so I'm embracing it for all the right reasons. I hope to do this for a long time."

Chapter 10
Nurture Your Relationships

"Each relationship nurtures a strength or weakness within you." - Mike Murdock

In the game of hockey, it's not always how well you play, but how well you work with others. In the game of life, it's not always what you know, but who you know.

Some of your toughest days on and off the ice will feel like you're stranded on an island, completely shut off from the rest of the world. Stuck between trying to handle it all on your own and not quite knowing which way to turn, you will find yourself in a vulnerable spot, left alone with your thoughts and secrets. Like fumbling for the keys while being chased in the dark, nerves quickly turn into anxiety and you start to lose control.

You're clearly not alone when it comes to having days like these. In fact, most coaches and sports psychologists will agree when we say that your toughest moments as a competitive athlete are often made up of battles you can't win alone. With nowhere to turn and no place to hide, sometimes the only way out of a downward spiral is by having someone at your side.

People care. Your family cares. Your teammates care. We care. Don't allow yourself to walk the path alone. Don't shut people out just because they may not totally understand you. Try talking to them instead. You don't have to reveal everything you're battling right away, you just need a chance to vent and explain yourself. Sharing what you're feeling, even to a lesser degree, is a key step in accepting what has happened and what you're going through.

If you can do this, whether they are truly dark days that keep you up at night, or you just have something small that's bothering you, it will develop a bond and create a level of trust with those that are willing to help you. It gives you an outlet and it helps you to build an all-important support group that will always be there to lift you up when you're feeling down.

On the flip side, the more you care about your teammates, your coaches, your mentors, and your followers, the more empathetic you will become. You will be a man or woman for others, instead of all for yourself. You will become more egoless and therefore less prideful. It will take some of the pressure off as well, because it's not all about you anymore.

Think about every single interview ever conducted with a hockey player making his NHL debut. They all say the same thing in slightly different ways.

"My family and a lot of other great people helped me along the way," they say. "I wouldn't be here without them."

Whether you like it or not, people are going to be a part of your life forever. You need people to care for you. You need to care for people. Hockey is the ultimate team sport, and many of your teammates will be friends for life. They will be there at your high school graduation, your college graduation, your wedding day, and even at your funeral.

With love as the foundation for all of your relationships in life and in hockey — love for the game, love for your teammates, a love of the daily grind — there is no such thing as losing.

Chapter 11
Evgeni Nabokov

Introduction: *One of the last of a dying breed, the goaltending community will forever remember and respect the narrow butterfly style that made Evgeni Nabokov one of the most successful Russian goaltenders of all time. This tale of bravery and adventure takes you back to the days of the Soviet Union, before Nabokov's native Kazakhstan was even considered an independent republic. At that time, hockey culture was very different; coming over to North America to play in the NHL was unheard of, especially for a goalie. But Nabokov would stop at nothing to pursue his dream. He would take that plunge and embrace all of the fear and uncertainty that came with it. Everything from the language barrier to the vastly different playing styles became real-life obstacles getting in the way of his rise to stardom with the San Jose Sharks. Through it all, steadfast he remained, until that memorable day of January 19, 2000. It was on that night where he would make 39 saves in his first NHL start for a 0-0 shutout tie against Patrick Roy and the Colorado Avalanche. Over 16 years later, "Nabby" now sits alongside some of the best in the NHL goaltending pantheon with a "Rookie of the Year" award (in 2001) and an impressive 353 wins in 697 total games.*

Goldman: Mike and I chose to conduct your interview a little differently than the others for a few reasons. First of all, your lengthy NHL career and durability in the league was legendary. Secondly, similar to your coaching counterpart in San Jose [Johan Hedberg], you're now seeing things from the other side. Thirdly, your Russian upbringing is a great insight for readers, as the cultural differences in goalie development can bring us a better perspective. With that in mind, how did hockey first enter your life as a child?

Nabokov: "I was very fortunate to grow up in a hockey family. My dad was a goalie, so as a kid, I spent a lot of time in the locker room with him. Any time he had a chance, he'd always bring me to practices or into the locker room after the game to see the guys. Right around age seven, I started skating like every other kid, but as a forward and a bit on defense. To be honest with you, I don't remember exactly how or when I first put the goalie pads on, but I think I was around nine years old. My mom didn't really want me to be a goalie, but my dad didn't care. He just wanted me to be happy. That's how I started."

Goldman: What was your early goalie or hockey training like as a kid in Russia?

Nabokov: "It wasn't too crazy, to be honest. In Russia, if you were a goalie, you had to be in great shape. But the goalies never did a lot of weights. We would do a lot of jumping and other things, but never weightlifting like the other guys. We never did that. In fact, sometimes instead of weight lifting in Dynamo or in my hometown, we would play tennis and work on our reactions with tennis balls. When I was even younger, I went to a summer camp once where we went swimming in the lake and then practiced in full gear, even though there was no ice on the outdoor rink. We'd just be out there in our gear and players would shoot high so we could work on our hands. Back then, the butterfly wasn't really used, so you'd go on one knee and kick the puck with an old-school skate save. We would work on that a bit, but the main thing was to work on our hands. We'd try to catch everything or steer everything to the corner. No rebounds. Doesn't matter how hard, how high, or how low it was, we'd steer it to the corner."

Goldman: What about your father? I know he was a goalie as well. Was it tough living up to certain expectations, or was he pretty carefree during your early playing days?

Nabokov: "He would criticize me a lot, actually. After every game in my hometown, we would walk back home and talk about the game the entire time. He was basically giving it to me every single time [laughing]. Even if I won a game 4-1, he would try to find what I did wrong in those games, so our house was always hockey, hockey, hockey. We talked hockey, we watched hockey. Sometimes I felt like it was too much, but I'm only realizing that right now. Back then, it was normal to me. When you're 12 years old and your dad talks to you about hockey, you talk about hockey. You can't really say anything else. You listened and you did it."

Goldman: What about when you started playing internationally and representing your country? Was there a lot of pressure on you at that time?

Nabokov: "In 1990, shortly before I turned 15, I made my first trip to Lake Placid. When you're making strides with the national junior team, it does become a big deal. You end up on a bit of a different path where you realize that maybe you can make hockey your future. But again, we never really talked about it. It's kind of like a process. You make it to the National team, you go, you play and have fun, then you come back. Nobody really talked about the importance of this or that. No, you just go play against the Czechs and Canada or the United States and you just want to win those games. You basically just prepared for the games and try to win them."

Goldman: All this was happening when the Soviet Union started to dissolve, right?

Nabokov: "I played for the Soviet Union's national junior team until 1992, when I was 17. Then it broke up from the Republic into the different countries. Since I was from Kazakhstan and it became its own country, I wasn't able to play for Team Russia anymore. By 1994, because of the separation, hockey in my hometown became very weak. We weren't in the same championships with Russia anymore, so that had a major impact on my city. But I got an offer from Dynamo Moscow and obviously I took it right away, because they were one of the top teams in Russia and it was a very famous organization. I was so happy."

Goldman: There was a major political, economic, and cultural transition in Russia at the time, which is something very unique to many other goalies. How did the contract with Dynamo change things for you?

Nabokov: "When I got there, the coach gave me a chance to grab the starting spot right away. Although I didn't play every single game, I played a lot, including in the playoffs. In my first year there, we won the Championship. In the second year, we won it again. In 1994, I also got drafted by the Sharks, but it was in the ninth round, so I was a low pick."

Goldman: When did you finally hear from the Sharks?

Nabokov: "I don't know if you remember the old Euro League, but all of the best clubs in Europe would play in a tournament every year with teams from Finland, Sweden, Germany, and Russia. We made it to the Finals one year, and that's when Wayne Thomas and John Ferguson came over to me and basically said that they wanted me to come play in North America."

Goldman: Is that when the reality of possibly becoming an NHL goalie finally hit you?

Nabokov: "Yes. I wanted to come over right away, but I was really scared, because I was in such a good spot with Dynamo. We won the Championship two years in a row and I was comfortable there. But when we had to make the decision with my parents and as a family, we decided that I would come over and try to make it to the NHL. If I wasn't going to make it, then I was going to come back to Russia."

Goldman: Why was that so scary for you?

Nabokov: "Can you imagine back in 1997 when Russian players just started coming over to North America? Nowadays, it's not a big deal at all. Kids are even speaking English in Russian schools now. But back in 1997, it was only five-to-six years since Russians first started coming over. It was very rare, and to be honest with you, we had no idea what to expect. Do we want to try for the NHL? Or do we want to stay and be comfortable right where we're at? I was already really comfortable, so the challenge was going to a new country where everything would be different. I thought I knew a bit of English, but it turned out I didn't [laughing]."

Goldman: What was that like for you? So many brand new things. What were your emotions like during that time?

Nabokov: "The biggest thing was learning to understand the coaches. Sometimes I just didn't get the coaches or understand exactly what they needed, what they wanted, or why I wasn't playing. That was the most frustrating part. Otherwise it was actually pretty good, because I think we had five or six Russian guys on the ice. We were pretty comfortable off the ice."

Goldman: How did you learn to communicate better with your coaches during that time?

Nabokov: "It was all about time. The first year was bad, the second year was a little better, and the third was better than that. I had to trust the process, and if I were to compare myself now to how I was back then, it's like day and night. I didn't say much and I never understood the team's system in the minors. I had no idea what the hell we were doing on the ice. But goalies could get away with that — it was easier back then. I never understood what we really did on our breakouts or how we played in the neutral zone. In Russia, you don't have similar formations. We never played like we do now with the Box, the Umbrella, or a 1-3 penalty kill."

Goldman: What advice would you give to a young Russian goalie prospect who has never been to the States before, but still aspires to play in the NHL one day? What can you tell him or her about the obstacles they may face when coming over to North America?

Nabokov: "I think the number one thing is the language. That will clear up a lot of obstacles. The rink is smaller too, so you have to understand what the coaches and players want from you. If you want to play, you have to know what the players are saying, so language is still the most important to me. Then you have to adjust your angles a little bit, but you have to work with your goalie coach on that, so everything still comes down to the language. Back then, it wasn't as robotic and technical at is today, so it was easier to just go out and play. Nowadays, everything has become so technical that on bad-angle shots, you have to do a Reverse-VH or a regular VH. But back then, it was pretty simple; you just covered the post. How you covered it? Nobody was really going to tell you exactly how to do it back then. You just covered the post."

Goldman: After landing on American soil, what was your first training experience like?

Nabokov: "The first year I got here, I remember the Sharks sent me to Minnesota to attend Warren Strelow's summer goalie camp. All of the Sharks goalies at the time were there, so I think there was a total of five of us. Warren was there with [former Sharks goalie coach] Wayne Thomas and they were working with us and some shooters."

Goldman: What was your first interaction with Warren Strelow like?

Nabokov: "The first time I saw Warren, I remember thinking, 'Oh boy, he's a much older guy!' He didn't skate on the ice, he would always walk around out there. So I was like, 'Wow, that's my coach?' But we started talking and we clicked right away. He was easy to communicate with, because he would explain everything in a way I could understand. We also had a translator there, so if I didn't understand something, he would explain to me what Warren said. But we didn't use him much, because we were just able to understand what was going on. We would work a lot on technique, angles, stuff like that. It was really interesting. We had a video camera set up and we'd watch ourselves after the session, which was pretty cool, because growing up in Russia, we never did video. Nobody was doing it. Whatever coach told you to do, you did it."

Goldman: After that summer training camp, did your nerves ramp up as you started to get those first pro games in North America?

Nabokov: "We started the season and my initial expectation was that I'd play a lot of games, but that wasn't the case at all. I only played like every third game or on the tail end of a back-to-back, so I really struggled. My numbers weren't good and I felt like my coach didn't trust me, so I wasn't comfortable to be honest with you, and I didn't really like it. I had signed a three-year deal and after the first year was over, I sat down and realized I had won two championships in Russia, but came over here to basically be a backup. But I talked with my agent and my family and decided to stay. I gave it one more try."

Goldman: How did things end up going in that second year?

Nabokov: "The second year was a little better. I think I had 26 wins and only 14 losses, so my numbers were better. But the playoffs came around and I didn't start, and I was pissed off again, because I didn't understand why. I got all upset over that, but when we lost the first game of the series, I was given a chance to play, and I went the rest of the way. We won that series and the next one as well, so things were getting much better. I felt like I was playing better."

Goldman: After your first taste of success in the playoffs, did the doors really start to open in San Jose? At that point everyone had to know that you were making waves.

Nabokov: "After the training camp in my third year, they told me I had to go to Cleveland in the IHL. I was surprised by that move, but they told me that was the only way I would play regularly, because we had a bit of a logjam in San Jose with Kiprusoff, Hedberg, Toskala, and Mike Vernon. With so many goalies in the organization at the time, I agreed to go to Cleveland. It turned out to be really good for me, because I played really well. It was a smarter game with some older guys in the league. I had a really good first half of the season and then all of a sudden in December, they traded Vernie and I got called up. They told me that I was going to stay for the rest of the season, so I was excited about that. I played a couple of games and everything went well."

Goldman: What changed for you in Cleveland in terms of your attitude?

Nabokov: "When I was in Cleveland, Warren was with me all the time. That's exactly where and when he and I really clicked. We did everything together. We drove together. We worked on the ice together. We talked about hockey together. My English was also getting better, so we were able to communicate on a much deeper level. Back then, I had no idea why he was with me so much. But now I know how things work. I know he was with me for a specific reason."

Goldman: During those two months in Cleveland, what did you learn about yourself?

Nabokov: "I don't know if I learned anything, but I was more relaxed, because I was playing a lot. Back when I was in Kentucky, I felt like I deserved to play, but it never happened. If you're not in a rhythm and you're not playing a lot, it's hard to figure out who you really are. I played really well in Russia and I was winning, but I came over here and had to start all over again. For me, that was the biggest struggle and toughest emotional grind. I never understood why I was only playing every third game, or only when my team was tired at the end of three games in three nights. I just felt like I wasn't given a fair opportunity to play, and I really struggled to cope with that."

Goldman: How did you overcome it? How did you continue to prove yourself?

Nabokov: "Well, Warren was in Kentucky a lot. He taught me to be patient and told me how sometimes that's the way things work in North America, because there are older guys with larger contracts. Then you have the younger guys that are drafted later and are still learning how to get to the NHL. My problem was that I thought I'd be a starter right away in the minors, because I came off three really good years in Russia. I felt like I was already a proven starter, or would at least get the opportunity to be a starter right away. I just didn't understand how things worked at the time. In my mind, that's what I wanted, and I never had it. So I was pissed off a lot, but Warren always told me to stay patient and things will work out. Just practice well, prepare well, and when you get the call, play well."

Goldman: After your short stint in Cleveland, you got called up to San Jose. You played in 11 games and notched your first NHL shutout. The next season, boom, you played in 66 games. You got what you wished for. Was there anything about that 66-game grind that surprised you?

Nabokov: "At the time, Steve Shields was the starter, but he sprained his ankle and it was a high sprain, so he was out for like four or five weeks. They gave me a chance, but I'm not sure I was actually the first on the list. I think they were waiting for Kipper to mature a little bit longer. He was there with Toskala and both were higher draft picks, but I was fortunate enough to grab the spot and never let go. [Head coach] Darryl Sutter was really good to me and he fit the coaching personality of what I grew up around. He was really hard but really direct. You knew exactly what he needed from you. He wouldn't bullshit around. Sometimes coaches have a conversation with you, but you don't really understand what the hell they want from you. With him, if he didn't like something, he'd let you know it wasn't good enough. Some games, I'd give up two or three goals and thought they weren't bad. But he'd come in and say, 'Hey, this is the NHL. I need those saves. I don't care how good those goals were, I need those saves.'"

Goldman: He held you accountable.

Nabokov: "Yeah. He was really good about that. I like when people are straight up. So I played a lot of games and after that, and everything else was history I guess [laughing]."

Goldman: Speaking of history, I wanted to ask you about a game you played in back when I was scouting the Colorado Avalanche. It was in 2010 in the first round of the Stanley Cup Playoffs. It was Game 3 of a tight series and Craig Anderson made 51 saves and totally stood on his head in a 1-0 OT win. The goal that was scored was on a really crazy play. Dan Boyle had the puck along the boards directly to your right. He turned and tried to fire the puck behind the net, but it deflected off Ryan O'Reilly and somehow it redirected and snuck between your body and the right post. I'm not sure if you remember that game.

Nabokov: "Yeah, oh yeah. I absolutely remember that game."

Goldman: As soon as the game ended, while everyone's going nuts and mobbing Anderson and O'Reilly, I'm watching you and wondering not only what in the hell just happened, but what torture you must have been dealing with at that moment. How did you move past something like that? I mean, it's a must-win playoff game, the Sharks were expected to win, and you had absolutely no control over that brutal bounce.

Nabokov: "Not only that, but after it happened, everybody started blaming me for looking at Dan Boyle the wrong way. It [the blaming] was so stupid, because it was just my natural reaction when he tried to throw the puck behind the net. As he was skating by me, we looked at each other wondering what the hell just happened. But the media turned everything on us, and one thing I can't get used to in the States is how the media can twist things around and say it in their own way. They never asked about it, but they turned it around and said I blamed Boyle for that. They were idiots. I never blamed him for that. Is it a weird situation? Absolutely. Is it a stupid weird goal? Yes, it is. That's why we looked at each other right afterwards! So both of us had to deal with that, because I had to go over to Boyle and made sure he knew I wasn't sitting there blaming him for that goal, or something like that. But obviously we were good and he understood. Within the team it was never a problem. We knew that we were better than them, and we knew we just had to get past Andy. He was really good in that series, so I knew I couldn't give up more than one or two goals."

Goldman: That's exactly how it panned out for you guys. Andy finally wore down, you stood your ground, and you guys went on to win the series.

Nabokov: "That's where the focus and belief in your teammates really comes into play. I think what's helped me a lot throughout my journey was something my dad always said, 'You have to focus and be more focused on the game than all the other B.S.' In Russia, I never had to face the media and that much coverage, and that was a good thing. Here, you have to deal with all that. If I was a young guy now, I'd hate it. All of this Twitter and Facebook stuff would drive me nuts. That's why to this day I still don't have any of it."

Goldman: For you specifically, how did you keep yourself focused day after day through so many games and grueling years with the Sharks? You guys were expected to win every year and you had all the talent to get it done.

Nabokov: "I always said in both San Jose and New York that I don't care what everybody else thinks, but I do care what my teammates, my coach, and my G.M. thinks. If those three are backing me up on everything and believing in me, I could care less what everybody else thinks. That kind of attitude helped me embrace the grind and move forward without any hiccups. It's so hard to win; if there are hiccups along the way, you have to bounce back and stay strong. You can't hang your head. I know we didn't win the Stanley Cup here in San Jose, but we didn't fall off the face of the Earth, either. We always stayed strong and stayed together and had great seasons. You see a lot of teams that play in the Finals and then struggle to make the playoffs the next year. But we were confident, and Doug Wilson provided confidence with the coaching staff and players. We were good enough, so we just had to try it the same way again. When Teemu Selanne won the Stanley Cup, I asked him what he thought the difference was between our teams and his teams. He looked at me and said, 'You wouldn't believe how much luck is involved in all of this.' So all things have to be working together. Be lucky, get hot at the right time — and that's including the goalie and forwards — the PK gets hot, then you need to get a lucky goal, a lucky bounce. All of this has to come together at the right time. If it does, you're going to win."

Goldman: Were you ever frustrated with anyone on the team? Were there any obstacles you faced, like certain guys that got under your skin, or the team not working as hard as they could have been? If so, how did you deal with the other pieces of the puzzle?

Nabokov: "I think I was extremely lucky to have such a good team in front of me for so many years. Since 1997, even before I was in San Jose, the team was getting better every year. We were accumulating more points, we won the President's Trophy, and we won Division titles. We were always making steps in the right direction and getting better than the previous season. Then I remember when Anaheim beat us that everyone was saying our season was bad. But now I'm looking back and I'm like yeah, if you consider Selanne, [Chris] Pronger, [Scott] Niedermayer, [Ryan] Getzlaf, [Corey] Perry, and [Chris] Kunitz are all on their team, you're going to say that they were underdogs? That's kind of funny to me [laughing]. We were first in our Conference and they were eighth, because for some reason they struggled throughout the regular season. They beat us in the First Round, but when you lose to that type of team, it's not embarrassing. It sucks to lose, but we always had to go through Detroit, Colorado, Dallas, St. Louis, all of those teams were unbelievable. Every year, it was a different obstacle. It's not easy to win, and it's a lot tougher than people make it out to be."

Goldman: In your final three years with San Jose, you rattled off three consecutive 40-win seasons. That's probably considered one of your best stretches. But I want to talk about what happened after that. You went back to Russia and played in the KHL, and shortly thereafter, you wanted

to come back to North America. Then there was a lot of self-imposed drama created by the media regarding the Detroit Red Wings and the New York Islanders. Was that one of the toughest grinds of your career?

Nabokov: "Yeah it was definitely a weird situation, because after I decided to part ways with the Sharks, I was hoping to sign quickly with another NHL team. By July 10, my agent said he didn't have much going on. Nobody put an offer on the table and everybody was playing the waiting game. Then the Russian team came on board and they obviously offered good money, so I had a meeting with my family to discuss it. I was afraid to wait until August or September, because we were probably going to get low-balled. I decided it was better to strike first and make my decision, so I signed in Russia. Everything started well, but my family realized that they had no social life out there. The kids just went to school and came back home, and even though they were in an English-speaking school, still, it was hard to put my kids and wife in that situation. Then there were also certain things I didn't really like about the hockey. So I started to realize that it was going to be hard for me to be there all four years. I didn't want to let this go on for much longer, because I felt like if I stayed there for the whole year, it was going to be awful hard to come back."

Goldman: And that's when you heard from Detroit.

Nabokov: "I actually had an opportunity to come back with another team that wanted me before Detroit, but they got caught up with the risky waiver rule and backed out in December. I really got screwed there, because I had already brought my family back over to the USA. So now I'm waiting, and it wasn't until late-January or February when I told my agent I was getting ready to shut it down until next season. Sure enough, Detroit calls and we make an agreement. Then [Islanders G.M. Garth] Snow steps in, steals me [laughing], calls me up, and says we need you and we want you to play right now. All of his goalies had been injured, so he needed me to play right away. He didn't realize that I hadn't skated for a month and didn't even work out for over two weeks, so I said not a chance, because if I get injured or have a couple of bad games due to being out of game shape, that's it. I won't be able to find another job."

Goldman: I could see how that was a really tough situation for you.

Nabokov: "Yeah, because he suspended me. I had a contract though, so next season I could come in 100-percent ready and give the team a chance to succeed. But once again, the media was making a big deal out of it, saying that I didn't like the Islanders and this and that. I said right away that it had nothing to do with the Islanders — the NHL is the NHL — and I respect every single team. But in that situation, a lot of people thought I was full of shit and that I was just saying the right things to get out of it. I had a meeting with Snow and the team owner and told them straight up, if you want me to play for your team, I will come next season. But right now, I'm not ready."

Goldman: Sure enough, they signed you and everything was fine the following season.

Nabokov: "We had three goalies at the time, and I think I was the third guy at the beginning of the season, but I eventually became a number one goalie again for three years."

Goldman: Since you were a little older and in a different stage of your career with the Islanders, did you find it was more of a grind to maintain your body and your game?

Nabokov: "Actually, no, I didn't really feel this way. But what was grinding me down was my groin situation. I had a bit of a groin issue throughout my career, but when I was younger, it wasn't as obvious. I'd miss four or five days of practice and then I'd be fine to play again."

Goldman: Yeah, you were playing so many games, it's pretty amazing. That's why I'm curious about your style. It seems like compared to guys who played a lot of games back then like Roberto Luongo and Marty Turco, to me, your style was such that it allowed you to play all of those games. You were way more economical with that narrow butterfly and your style may have allowed you to be so durable over all those years.

Nabokov: "Just think, Marty Brodeur played a similar style. He played a lot on his feet and played up to age 40 as well. I don't think it really depends about this style or that style, it depends how you make the saves. You have guys now like Martin Jones or Braden Holtby, those guys make the game look so easy. And then you have the other goalies who are like the Pekka Rinne's and Jonathan Quick's; those guys that do so many different moves in a game. I just had a conversation with my goalies and they said, 'Jeez, if we played like Quick, we'd be dead by the end of the game.' Quick is the only one who can play that style. You can't teach another goalie that style. To each his own. In regards to me being more economical, my goal was simple. If you make the game look easy, it's usually easier on your body."

Goldman: What about those final few seasons in New York and Tampa Bay?

Nabokov: "Later on in New York, I don't know exactly why, but I started having tightness around my left leg all the time. To this day it's still a bit of a mystery. We tried everything and it was getting better, but after a few months, it would come back. So maybe it's age, because you're 37-38-39 [laughing]. That half-season in New York, I think I played 40 games out of 42 or 48."

Goldman: In your three years in New York, you played 42, 41, and then 40 games respectively. That's a lot of action at your age.

Nabokov: "After the shortened season, I started to have the groin problems again. By that time I was 38. I felt like I was still doing the same things I was before in terms of being in shape, but something I was doing was wrong. Maybe it was too much conditioning or jumping, or maybe I just had to slow down and rest a bit more. I started doing more massages and a little bit of acupuncture. But still, when you're 38 and you have groin problems, you can imagine what the G.M. starts thinking."

Goldman: That leads to my next question, which is kind of when you started to realize the end was in sight.

Nabokov: "Well, the G.M. automatically started saying how he liked my game and that I was playing well, but if I got injured, he'd need a goalie he can trust behind me. Unfortunately every time I got injured, the team struggled. So that was the situation. I think that's what also put me and the whole team in a bad spot. If I was injured for two weeks and the team went 2-7, then it was a problem. I knew that, and I saw that the end was coming. I was 38 and playing a lot, so I knew it was going to come."

Goldman: Now that we've gone through some different obstacles in your career, from your perspective, try and define the grind. How do you put that into simple words for younger goalies? What does it mean to you?

Nabokov: "It's hard work every single day and every single practice. You can't take a practice off. It's easy to do well when you're winning and having fun. But it's harder when you lose three or four in a row and you have to put work into your game. To me, that's when the grind really kicks in — when you've lost a few in a row and you know you have to win the next game. It's so competitive. If you can't make key saves at key times in key situations, you're not going to go far. Sometimes it could be a breakaway or a 2-on-0, it doesn't matter what type of play it is, you have to make the save. It's hard, and that's when the grind kicks in, when the expectations are so high every single night, and then you also have to carry those same expectations with you every single day."

Goldman: Pretty incredible ride, that's for sure. I know things didn't work out great for you in Tampa Bay, but I was really happy when San Jose signed you ceremoniously to retire as a Shark. That must have been a cool moment. But a bit selfishly, I want to close this up with a little bit about Strelow and your start in the coaching side of things. Things that he may have said to you, or anything about his influence that resonates with you about his coaching and how it is translating over to your work with the Sharks goalies.

Nabokov: "Warren didn't care if I got a shutout or gave up five goals the night before, he always wanted to work on something. I think his ability to identify what I needed, that's what he was so great at. I remember Warren had three things that he wrote down for me, and it's still with me. I actually have it right here in front of me. All the time, he talked about your foundation. He said your foundation is going to carry you through the grind and for your entire career. If you have a great foundation, even if you don't feel well, you can still have a decent game and give your team a chance to win. Under the foundation, a lot of things go into it. His number one thing was the repetition. Sometimes we would do the same drills all the time, because even if you're really good at it and things are going well, you still have to continue to do those drills. My feet were the key to my game, so I would continue to work on my feet a lot. Then came the glove saves and work with the stick. We would work on those fundamental skills every single day. The second thing he wrote was to stay focused. Those two things were exactly what my dad talked about when I was growing up. He was building my foundation when I was a kid, and then Warren was building it when I was a professional. I was so fortunate to have two great people involved in building my foundation. The third thing Warren wrote and always told me was to have fun. And that's the most important part for the goalie. The fun always has to be there."

Goldman: That's amazing stuff, and I can't wait to share it with every goalie involved in USA Hockey and the Warren Strelow Mentoring Program. It's not always easy when you're dealing with the stress and pressure, but it always comes back to love over fear.

Nabokov: "You really have to learn to look at it that way. The older I was getting, the more fun I was having. When you're younger, you're really concentrated on making the team or playing great every night. But later on when you do make it, you need to learn how to enjoy playing. I've watched Jaromir Jagr for years. There's no way he can play right now if he's not enjoying it. Not a chance, right? So it's the same thing. You have the foundation, you have the focus, now enjoy it. Those three things — that's what Warren Strelow taught me about goaltending."

Chapter 12

Remove the Rose-Colored Glasses

"If you want to be successful, you must respect one rule. Never lie to yourself." - Paulo Coelho

The toughest enemy you face as a goaltender is often yourself. Trapped inside your own mind, it can be difficult at times to escape the dangers and perils of your own self-deception.

One of the driving forces behind this self-deception is the fact that goalies are expected to be perfect. But in today's game, which is filled with imperfect moments and bad bounces, even a tiny mistake or unfortunate bounce can lead to bitter failure. Truth be told, there's simply no room for error anymore. As the old goaltending adage goes, if you can see the puck, you should stop it. And even if you don't see it, many coaches and parents still expect you to always stop it.

The unrealistic demands placed on a goaltender's shoulders continue to rise, but not just at the NHL level. Even eight-year-olds are being scoffed at, benched, and derided by ignorant coaches that don't know any better. Parents exhibit embarrassing behavior and show visible anger when their son or daughter bombs against a rival opponent. The amount of pressure young kids face today, due in part to an obsession of winning tournaments and games, is totally out of control.

As a result, many young goalies are burning out way too soon. They don't want to be singled out as the reason for losing, or the reason why their parents are disappointed with a performance. When a goalie plays for sheer enjoyment, but is suddenly tossed into his or her first competitive environment, they may begin to struggle with the idea that they must satisfy the expectations of coaches, parents. They are not playing for their own happiness, but to meet the unrealistic demands of everyone around them.

Once you're older and you know better, instead of trying to meet the expectations of others, you have to meet your own rising expectations. As a result, when you're left alone with nothing but your own thoughts and you're forced to look in the mirror, it takes honesty to accept your flaws and the failures that have been done and are still to come. But if you're not disciplined, or if your ego is getting in the way, you'll let your guard down and begin to lie to yourself. So the sooner you realize it's happening, the sooner you can begin to fight that temptation.

Therefore, all goalies (and parents!!) must learn to remove the rose-colored glasses and see themselves for who they really are. Be willing to admit that there are areas of your game that need improving. Your rebound control can always be better. You can be more flexible. You can have better sleep and eating habits. By saying these things, you can accept any and all weaknesses with an obedience to learn from them. This form of honesty will help break the chains that bind you from growth and maturity. This also allows you to not only trust yourself, but trust others as well.

Former Dallas Stars goaltender Marty Turco gave readers some great insight on this topic in *The Power Within*. When asked about handling the highs and lows of an NHL season, he explained how seeing things for what they really were allowed him to quickly move past the losses and stay level-headed after the wins.

When Turco would come back to the rink following a bad game, he would watch the game tape and realize he wasn't as bad as he originally thought. When he did the same thing following a good game, he would watch the game tape and realize he wasn't as great as he originally thought. The lesson, he said, was that things are never as good or as bad as they initially seem.

In a position like goaltending, where much of your success will forever be tied to wins and losses, always try to aim your moral compass in the right direction and be as honest with yourself as possible, even if that means admitting you're not playing good enough, you're not working hard enough, or you're not preparing the right way.

It's totally fine to admit you're wrong or that you're struggling, but it's not always easy to do so. If you constantly deflect your faults onto other people or situations, if you blame others for your mistakes, or if you cannot take ownership of them, you will always be chasing your true identity.

A single lie discovered by others is enough to make them doubt everything you say or do for the rest of your life. The same thing can happen within yourself. Lie to yourself too many times, and you begin to lack self-belief. This is where you must be so careful with your actions and decisions, because in order to succeed as a goalie, above all things, you must be able to trust every major choice you make and every little step you take.

Chapter 13
Mitch Korn

Introduction: *Undoubtedly regarded as one of the best goalie coaches of all time, Mitch Korn is on a level of genius that only a few men and women in the history of pro sports have ever achieved. In fact, let's just name some of the most legendary coaches in basketball, football, and baseball: Red Auerbach, Phil Jackson, John Wooden, Vince Lombardi, Scotty Bowman, Joe Torre, John Madden. Now ask yourself this question: "What do they all have in common?" For one, an ability to motivate and get the best out of others. Two, an ability to see technical or tactical problems before they arise and have an effective and proper solution. And thirdly, every legendary sports coach understands that their athletes are first and foremost people. Of course there are many other traits that matter, but there's no denying that these three clearly belong in the lexicon of coaching greatness. Proof that Korn belongs in this echelon is in the numbers. His success with goalies like Braden Holtby, Pekka Rinne, Dominik Hasek, Tomas Vokoun, Steve Shields, and so many others, is everlasting. Since joining the Capitals, plenty of positive press has been dished out about his personality and profession, but not many people know anything about Mitch Korn's less glamorous side of life. In this candid interview, you'll get a pretty hefty dose of the real-life grind of an NHL goalie coach, but with all of the passion and energy that we've come to admire from the one we affectionately call Goalie Yoda.*

Valley: We called this book "Embracing the Grind" for obvious reasons, but readers will learn that a lot of the goalies we interviewed don't see the hard times as a grind, because they're still having fun. But if you look at what we go through as NHL goalie coaches, it's pretty unbelievable. Every season for us is a *vicious* grind, and then on top of that, you

go from there right into your goalie and defensemen camps, which run all summer long.

Korn: "The guys in Nashville tell me that my good friend and replacement Ben Vanderklok says, 'How in the hell did Mitch do this for 25 years?' The new one I hear from Benny is, 'Now I finally understand why you made me do this a certain way.' It's because that's the way it works best [laughing]. But when you're not in that world, you don't get it. Yes, it is a grind, but winning certainly helps."

Valley: I talked to a reporter yesterday and he mentioned that many NHL and AHL goalie coaches are getting turned off by it. He said that a reason why a lot of guys want the NHL gig is just for the track suit, but the guys are just so mentally and emotionally burned out, there's a lot more turnover.

Korn: "It's very hard. In a lot of ways, goalie coaches are scapegoats. I say that, because we get stuck having to justify everything the goalie does. At times in the past, I'd sit upstairs with the General Manager and he would ask, 'Why did the goalie do that?' I'd think to myself, 'I'm sitting way up here! I can't tell you why, I can only guess.' I always assumed it was a rhetorical question [laughing]. I think to myself, 'Does he really want an answer?' I have to find a way to give him an answer. Every goal is a bad goal if it's an *important* goal. If you're dealing with the guy in charge of the penalty kill and they score a goal, it's not the penalty kill, it's the goalie! It's always the goalie. So we're defending them, yet we're managing and coaching them, too. We provide the tough love when we need to. We try not to let them off the hook too often. We try not to enable them or dis-able them. We also have to maintain their confidence, because without confidence, they can't play. We're dealing with so many variables at the same time. Having said all of that, I have been very lucky. Over the years, I have not gotten very much grief from the guys I worked with, whether it was in Nashville or now in Washington. But I've heard from other coaches how difficult it can be at times."

Valley: Isn't it crazy? A lot of guys just can't handle it.

Korn: "Here's the thing. For the guys that played in the league — the Rolosons and the Hedbergs and the Ranfords — it's way easier for them to have *played* the game than it is to have *coached* the game. They have more control when they play. It's easier to play and they actually enjoyed playing more than coaching, because playing is way less of a time commitment."

Valley: As a player, you also don't see all the behind-the-scenes stuff.

Korn: "Well, they just don't work that hard when they play, at least not in terms of total hours on a given day. For those of us that didn't play in the league, I think we enjoy *coaching* in the NHL more than the guys that *played*, because it's our only way *into* the league. I think the guys that *played* actually enjoy it less for all the different kinds of pressures they face; all the things they can't control, like where they sit during a game. They also don't like all of that grief and scrutiny directed toward their goalies. But having not played in the league, I think I appreciate it more."

Valley: Yeah, and as a coach, then you start to get over-protective.

Korn: "We get attached to our guys. We tend to want to protect them, because we understand what truly went on behind the scenes. I mean, every night when you're watching the highlights, somebody scores a goal when the goalie is in the Reverse [the RVH stance on the post]. You hear it mentioned every morning, 'Another bad goal. Another one from a bad angle. Another one on the short side. Another one that somehow leaked in. Another one over his shoulder. Why doesn't he just stand up?' But of course as coaches we sit here and think, 'If the goalie stood up, there'd be twice as many goals against,' right? But they don't know that, and we don't really see that style anymore, so we can't prove it."

Valley: If you think about your own personal grind as an NHL goalie coach in the 1990s, 2000s, and right now, what has changed and how would you explain it to people? Obviously it's time, right? It's the amount of time that you now put into the craft that people really don't see. You literally jump into it in August, you're underwater, and then all of sudden you pop your head out of the water and it's May. You look at it and say, "What the heck just happened?" You get back from a trip at 2:00 or 3:00 in the morning, you're back at the rink by 7:00 or 7:30 that same morning, and you just keep going. There's no questions about resting or anything like that, you just literally go non-stop.

Korn: "You're right. I would describe it as all-encompassing. I say it is a life*style* and it is not a choice once you're in it. You can do it the *right* way, or you can do it the *easy* way. Because the right way is *not* easy. When you and I talk about the right way, it's what *we both* believe, even though some teams don't do it that way. It's about building the correct structure like we installed in Nashville and that Benny [Vanderklok] has continued, and like we installed in Washington. It's where an NHL goalie coach can pull most of his goalie coach strings. That means we are intimate to what's going on with the goalies in the AHL, the ECHL, and all our prospects. As the NHL goalie coach, you don't just coach two goalies. You should be the key contact point and supervisor to the assistant goalie coach. We are working with the number-two guy and we're making schedules for both of us to go to the AHL and the ECHL. Maybe it's some amateur scouting, maybe it's some free-agent scouting, maybe it's some prospect scouting. Maybe it's watching a drafted guy that you have to go see before we decide to sign him. We are doing all of that. [AHL goalie coach] Scott Murray and I work together on all of these things. We are the ones watching all of the game video that our current goalies play. His job is to cut it up and share it with me. His job is to coach the minor league goalies with that video in order to help them improve. My job is to do the same thing with the NHL goalies, but I'm also watching his [Murray's] videos and monitoring what the minor league guys are doing, so I'm constantly communicating with them as well. As the NHL goalie coach, my job is to help the minor league goalie coach get better. A lot of NHL goalie coaches just don't communicate enough with their minor league guys, but I talk to Scott every day and I text the minor league guys frequently. Scott and I start working in October on projecting who might fill our open spots for the next season, and then we begin to accumulate and watch that video also. Together, we are a true Goalie Department. Besides all of that, technology and social media provides us with an enormous amount to read and watch."

Valley: We talk about the amount of workload we have, but what about the personal stresses that you've felt as an NHL goalie coach? What kind of weight do you carry on your own shoulders?

Korn: "I've been at this 25 years, so I'm pretty good at letting go. I don't get too high, I don't get too low. I try very hard not to feel the pressure of the game, especially when things are tight. You're sitting upstairs and you don't have any control, so it's natural to have a little anxiety and feel the pressure at that point."

Valley: It's an emotional roller coaster.

Korn: "It's funny. We joke that the next game starts when we've finished the beer to celebrate winning the previous game. So you're never done. You're always looking at the next game, the next week, the next, and the next, and the next. On any given night, we have to get closure, which takes about two hours after a game for our goalie. It's either going to be with a marked-up video that we share with them, or it will be a sit-down, face-to-face with that goalie. Everybody now has some of their own analytics; things that you think are important that you want to track for trends, strengths, and weaknesses. So you also have to do all of those things before you can move on to the next game. The thing that's crazy now is the *amount* of pre-scouting that we do for the opposing goalie. If you don't know who's going to play, sometimes you have to do that for two goalies. You're grabbing clips of their tendencies, strengths, weaknesses — the shootout has become monumental in that preparation — and then getting all of that video together in a way that will make your players actually watch it. That means you get a little fancier every year, you add another graphic here, you add a little of this, you add a little of that. All of these things take a lot of time and a lot of effort. You know it, I know it, and it's like Groundhog Day, because you're doing it over and over again."

Valley: Eighty-two times in less than eight months.

Korn: "You play St. Louis today and did all of that work, and then you look up and see that you play them again in two weeks. You want to do all of that same work again with all new video, so you have to spend time finding all new stuff. We don't like using the same video clips twice, because we want to do it right. So you're doing the pre-scouting, you're doing the post-game stuff, you're doing the minor league stuff, and you're helping the assistant goalie coach get better, too. I've always said that one part of my job is to help the minor league and junior prospect goalies get to the NHL. If I have to do that, then I have to help my assistant goalie coach get to the NHL as well. That means I have to teach him and train him, too. If I'm the lead goalie coach in the organization, then I need to train and coach my assistant. I did it with you, I did it with Benny, and I'm hoping to do it now with Scott Murray."

Valley: Was there ever a time where you almost felt like you were going to completely break down? Did you ever have to take some emotion out

of it? You said over time you learned how to stay even-keeled, but was there ever a moment in time where you almost broke apart at the seams?

Korn: "You know what? I've been lucky. After my first year when I had a leave of absence from Miami University and was in Buffalo full-time, I have always literally had three full-time jobs. I've had the NHL, and then for 17 of these 25 years in the NHL, I've also had my job at Miami University. I've also done summer camps for the past 20 years, so I've never been totally dependent — to feed my family and pay my mortgage — on my NHL coaching gig. Gerry Meehan [the GM that hired me in Buffalo] once said to me, 'Don't give up your day job.' That was a saying that stuck with me, so I've never coached scared. I've never felt that if I lost my job, I'd have to completely relocate my family and myself, which is a lot of pressure when you're the breadwinner, when you have children, and when you're trying to survive. Due to these different streams of income and having been in a position to manage these things all at one time, I never felt boxed in."

Valley: If you look at it from a coaching perspective, you're 100-percent right. I think you're actually a better coach when you're not fully dependent on the team that you're working for.

Korn: "You know what else makes you a better coach? Not being there with the NHL goalie every minute of every day. In all my years in Buffalo and in my first 10 years in Nashville, I've learned what happens when I come in and out. After being gone, when you come back, they're glad to see you. You could see new things that you couldn't see when you were there every day. You were refreshed and you felt better. You had a change of scenery. It was all better. In my last six years in Nashville when I lived there and was there virtually every day, I found I was in some ways less productive. You have to know when to get out of the way. You could easily get tired of each other. If you don't have those breaks, the goalie does not learn to manage his own game."

Valley: And as a result, you start over-coaching.

Korn: "The good news is, having done this well into my 50's, I know when to get out of the way. If I was 42 again right now, I would not know how to get out of the way. I'd be overbearing, micro-managing, and driving them crazy. Now in Washington, I built my current contract around being able to get away for a period of time, to give the goalies some breathing room and space. I also did it in order to help make them accountable for managing their own game, which I think is extremely valuable and something that's lost, because goalie coaches are around too much, and they hover. But because of the pre-scout stuff that we've done — not every team does as much as you and I have done, and I think I did more than you did just because of the video assistance I was provided — we get boxed in and we're forced to be there, because we end up needing to do all of these other things instead of just coaching our goalies."

Valley: So if you say that time away helps the goalies get through the grind, don't you think it's good for us as coaches as well? It's good for us to get away and have other interests, because all of that time off helps you get through the coaching grind.

Korn: "I don't think the teams are worried about coaches in that way. The thought is, 'If other assistant coaches can't get away, why should the goalie coach get away?' The coaches I work with in Washington don't always understand when I go away. But yes, there is a value to the goalies managing their own game and there's value to us getting away, even if it's just to go scouting or to help out the other minor league guys. I think that separation is good. When you return, they're glad to see you, and there's usually a boost in their play."

Valley: I totally agree. I feel like there are more and more young goaltenders that can't manage their own game if a goalie coach isn't standing right next to them. And that's not good, because when we sit up in the press box, we can't manage their game. They have to do it themselves.

Korn: "The problem is, if you do it right, which includes the pre-scouting and the post-game stuff, and because it can't all be done remotely, you get boxed-in for more of the 'non goalie coaching' things, so it's harder to get away. My favorite part of coaching goalies is *coaching goalies*. That's the time when we're on the ice, we're doing our goalie stuff, and we're doing all of the things that we're paid to do! It's sitting with them and watching video, or making a video to help make them better. I feel like I'm really only coaching 30-percent of the time now. In the 90's, especially before the digital age, it was like 90-percent."

Valley: Yeah, so it's really changed.

Korn: "There's still guys in our league that just do that, and go home. There's a changing of the guard for that reason around our league, and that's one of the reasons why some of the incomes aren't where they need to be. It's perceived that the NHL goalie coach works with two guys and that's all they do. In some cases, that *is* all they do. Often the number-two goalie guy reports to the team's head of player development. There's not a lot of pre-scouting. They're not involved in the amateur selections. They don't worry about the minor league goalies. And you know that's a big portion of this league, right? So I believe strongly that the head goalie coach — the guy at the NHL level — is actually meant to be the Director of a Goalie Department."

Valley: Let's say you're sitting at a table and across from you is a young Mitch Korn in his first year coaching in the NHL. What do you tell him about the grind and the journey he will go on? What's the best piece of advice you could give a young Mitch Korn?

Korn: "I've given this to other guys that get this kind of job, including Scott: It's not worth defending your goalie and arguing with the rest of your coaching staff. For harmony and for mental health, just tell everybody, 'You're right, it's a bad goal. I'll take care of it,' and move on."

Valley: That's a really good answer, but that's the answer you're telling others. Now I want you to get even more personal. What do you tell the young Mitch Korn about the ride you're about to go on for the next 25 years?

Korn: "Having not played in the league, my ride is way different. I said that at the beginning of this interview; I believe those of us that aspire to play in the NHL and never got there embrace this grind way more than the guys that *did* play in the NHL and are now coaching here. I've also been lucky, so lucky. I've had a chance to coach some unbelievable goalies! I think if I gave young Mitch Korn a piece of advice, the very first thing I would say is to develop a relationship with each. Develop trust with each. People are more important than pucks. Everybody's an individual. Everybody plays differently. It's a people game. Coach people. In addition, attach yourself to a great head coach if you can. I was way luckier to find Barry Trotz than he was to find me."

Valley: Those are both awesome answers, but I want to dig even deeper, because those answers were specific to coaching. How about personally — your lifestyle and family?

Korn: "Well, what I tell young Mitch Korn is that hockey — this lifestyle — can provide a great living, great challenges, and great experiences. But it can also be very destructive in a lot of ways. No question it can be destructive to family, to hobbies and to health, because of the time demands, the pressures, and the travel. That is a price you have to choose to want to pay, having not played in the league, to be coaching in the league. Like most people, you don't believe it [the destructive nature] will ever happen to you, and then lo and behold, it does. I give married couples that I know like Barry Trotz unbelievable credit for still being in fantastic marriages and relationships. There's a lot of guys where that's just not the case. The volume of divorces or problems are pretty significant. It's the nature of the beast."

Valley: You know we've had some of those conversations many times.

Korn: "We have both been affected, and you know what? Many wives may know what they're getting into, but it's still hard for them, especially if they work and have kids. Certainly mine did. I get it. Every situation is different as to why things go south. I would imagine if I was around every day, they might have gone south quicker, who knows."

Valley: I recently talked to a friend and coach who was hired by a new NHL team. He called me and said, 'Vals, I went in and told my kids about it, and they're just not happy.' That's a tough thing for anyone to hear, but like many NHL coaches, he has found great opportunities and jobs going from team to team for nearly a decade. That's successful in

terms of hockey, but we suddenly forget that the grind involves our families. It involves our wives, kids, girlfriends, and it's your family, your mom, your dad. It's almost like you have to say to yourself, are you ready for this? Are you ready for this journey?

Korn: "When you get into this, you really don't know what you don't know. Neither does the family. Everyone is excited and it's a dream come true. But then there are 'side effects' to everything. Often there's more social pressure on the families of coaches, especially if you don't win enough. Remember, almost everyone in our profession gets fired at some time or another. I missed a lot of my daughter growing up."

Valley: It's kind of the same for goalies. What did you witness with guys like Hasek, Rinne, Vokoun, Mason, and now Holtby? How were they able to get through it? People on the outside don't see it, so what is it that the most successful guys have done or have in their personalities that help them get through the grind?

Korn: "Simply, they love to play. You and I have both coached guys that love to get *paid*, and then there are guys that love to *play*. They love to be on the ice. They love to go out there for an optional skate. They love the concept of competing. They love being the key guy. They thrive on it, they embrace it, they love that battle and that journey. For the best guys, it's not work. For some of the guys that aren't the best or burn out, it's work."

Valley: Have you had guys before that you feel didn't love the game?

Korn: "Absolutely. They love being in the locker room, the lifestyle, the travel, and all of those things, but they don't love to practice, train or play. We've both coached them! When you see that, you know they won't break the glass ceiling if they don't love it."

Valley: What have you seen in Braden Holtby? Is there anything on the emotional side that you've seen that have helped him break through that ceiling?

Korn: "Braden Holtby is very cerebral, dedicated, and passionate. He really had the mental game together long before I met him with the help of a guy in Edmonton named John Stevenson. That's what John does for a living now. He's a sports psychologist and works with a variety of Canadian Olympic teams and Canadian athletes. He introduced Braden very early to the things that were important mentally. That is not only the mind, it is the mind's ability to manage emotions, and it's hard sometimes to get your emotions in check, no matter how mentally tough you may be. I will say that John did a magnificent job and Braden did an equally magnificent job in absolutely learning that side of it. When I met Braden at age 25, he already had a lot of that under control, and I think that really helped make it easier to create the physical changes that were required. Nowadays, Braden's two kids have become a great 'escape' from the grind for him."

Valley: It's funny, there's so many things we can dig into here between goalies and coaches. But we all know the grind is full of emotional ups and downs. What you've put into a nice little box here for readers, and I absolutely love this, is that it really comes down to a couple of simple things, and the most important is that you have to love the game. If you love the game, that will help you get through anything.

Korn: "I mentioned it's a people game, so you have to love them, too. You have to really like the goalies you're working with, and they have to enjoy us too! You need to have a sense of humor. But don't confuse a sense of humor for being soft. Don't confuse it for not expecting somebody to maximize their effort. You also need to enjoy the rest of the coaching staff, because you spend so much time with them. You must enjoy being around those guys. I have been so lucky being able to survive 18 years with Barry Trotz. In my first seven years in Buffalo, I worked for four head coaches. That was difficult, but it was my first seven years in the NHL, so it was still new and I always embraced being there. But as the grind got tougher and the workload and pressure increased, the relationships that I had with the coaching staff, especially in Nashville, needed to get stronger. Sometimes you don't want to let yourself down, but in my situation, I didn't want to let Barry and the rest of the staff down. I worked with him, Brent Peterson, and David Poile from the day we started in Nashville; 16 straight years. I have been with Lane Lambert a long time through thick and thin as well. There was never a personal agenda. You don't really find that anywhere."

Valley: Never.

Korn: "I was very lucky that they became family. When I got divorced, my daughter grew up, my dad died, and now my mom's getting old. They became my extended family and I needed that."

Valley: So you have to love the game. It doesn't matter if you're a PR guy, a goalie coach, a head coach, a goalie, whatever.

Korn: "Absolutely. There are guys we know that play, but only because they're good at it, not because they love it. They play because they always played, and they don't know what else to do. They do it because their dad expects them to do it, and that's certainly true at the younger age levels. They do it because they have no other way or idea of how to make money. But sometimes it's for all the wrong reasons."

Valley: And then it never works out.

Korn: "Rarely does."

Valley: The other thing you said is that you have to love the people you're around. You have to love working with your goalies and the staff. The other thing you said you learned very early that you can't take things too seriously, because that will beat you down.

Korn: "Absolutely. Everything runs off my back. I joke that there's not a single thing you can say to me that will offend me. Everybody is so sensitive and gets offended so easily. We protect our areas. I've learned not to worry about protecting my area — the goalies — anymore. Since I don't need to protect them, there's nothing you can say about my heritage, my size, my weight, or my nose that's going to offend me. I have thick skin, and you must have thick skin in this game to play it and to coach goalies, because the game will eat you up if you don't."

Valley: What does Mitch Korn do, or what does Mitch Korn want to do, to relax away from the game? Anything that has nothing to do with the game.

Korn: "There's not much time for that. Remember, for me, it's Caps all season and then camps all summer. My friends joke that I have no hobbies — I certainly don't play golf. So I have no idea what I'm going to do when I retire. If I need to relax, I will tell you this: I like television and I hate hockey games [laughing]. I'd rather watch HBO, Family Guy, or Seinfeld than a hockey game on a Tuesday night. But you have to watch hockey sometimes for your job! More than anything though, I love the water, like big lakes or oceans. I don't necessarily want to go in them, I just like to look at them. It's one of the only things that takes me from 90 RPM's to 10 RPM's. I just love to look at the water. Each summer we do a goalie camp in Duluth, Minnesota. We stay right on Lake Superior and I look out on the lake and I melt. I also go on vacation at the ocean on Hilton Head Island. I just love it."

Valley: It's funny you say that, because I knew that answer and obviously that's why you have a place in Florida. You go a thousand miles per hour, but I know there's a piece of you that wants to just be able to say, "I want to have my week of rest." Everybody needs that, and the times I've heard in your voice where you're at peace with yourself is always when you're close to the water.

Korn: "And that's certainly not in a bathtub."

Valley: No, exactly. It's not a bathtub in Detroit at a Marriott [laughing].

Korn: "No, it's not. Unfortunately, I don't live on the water, but I can drive there in 20 minutes. But I am rarely at my Florida home."

Valley: Well, Mitch, this was awesome. The insights you're giving by once again sharing your experiences is really inspiring and so valuable for readers. The feedback we get from having you in the first book is awesome. If I look back, it's probably given me the most "good feeling" inside of me, just doing something that has a positive impact.

Korn: "We're a lot alike, Mike. We were goalies, I've always said this, and I think it's even in *The Power Within* chapter. The best goalies have a burning desire to make a positive difference in a game. Well, now we're goalie coaches, but that burning desire to make a positive difference in other people's lives still hasn't gone away! We both have that burning desire, and that is why the feeling is so cool for you, because you and Justin have achieved that with these books. That is what my career is built on. What I've done, the people I've been fortunate enough to be around and influence — in pro hockey, in summer camps, at Miami University — are the things I am most proud of. It's the people; it all goes back to the people. I want to make a positive difference on those people's lives. I want to help them be better, help them reach their goals, and help them not only understand the hockey stuff, but the life lessons that come from hockey."

Chapter 14
STRIVE FOR BALANCE IN LIFE

"Man maintains his balance, poise, and sense of security only as he is moving forward." - Maxwell Maltz

In the first chapter of *The Power Within*, we created a graphic to help readers and goalies visualize the importance of balance in life. Through the use of a Venn diagram, we explained how the best way to have long-term success is by striving to exhibit the three pillars of elite goaltending — Mind, Body, and Spirit — as equally as possible.

We specifically said "striving" instead of "achieving" above, because we know that having true balance is a life-long battle. Some days you have it, some days you don't, and even when you do, there's no guarantee it will lead to success. Managing the emotions that arise from striving for balance, and having the discipline to sustain it, is a big part of the goaltender's daily grind.

Routine is easy. It's automatic and a programmable part of life. There's not much thought or energy required to process your daily exercises and tasks. But discipline is different. Discipline must be managed and maintained and honed every day of your life. It doesn't always come automatically, especially when you're tired, depressed, uncomfortable, or stressed. You have to work hard at it, even though there will never be a time in life where you have truly mastered it.

Beyond working on your self-discipline, one way to strive for better balance in life is to take an interest in other things. We've heard this a million times before; coaches stress the importance of being a multi-sport athlete, teachers urge you to join a club at school, and senior advisors recommend you to consider what degree you want before you begin applying to colleges.

Even then, when so much of your routine and your daily life is spent trying to be the best hockey player you can be, it comes as no surprise that you still find it difficult to do anything else. For the most part, you wake up, go to the rink, go to school, go back to the rink, go home, do some homework, and go back to sleep.

You're still leading a fun and exciting life, but you're mostly stuck in the same ring. So how do we break that mold? One way to do this is by going to new places as much as possible. That could be walking to a new park, hanging out with an old friend, or taking an hour to bike or hike in the opposite direction you're used to going.

Simply put, changing your environment will change your perspective. Seeing different things in different places brings about different experiences and opportunities to meet new people, learn new things, and see yourself in a different light. By doing this, you're no longer thinking about hockey 24-7. Doing so means you're slightly less of a function of your usual routine. This will in turn help you develop more confidence, awareness, and most importantly, better balance.

Sometimes you just have to get away from what you know in order to learn more about what you don't know. The more you can do this, the easier it becomes to not only strive for better balance, but to hang on to it for longer periods of time.

Chapter 15
Drew MacIntyre

Introduction: *Behind an impressive 13-year pro hockey career, Drew MacIntyre has developed a strong reputation as one of the most serviceable and reliable depth goaltenders of all time. From the Toledo Storm to the Toronto Marlies to the Rockford IceHogs (and many more teams in between), he's the perfect reflection of a man who has fully embraced all of the emotional and physical grinds that come with being a career minor leaguer. He's lived out of suitcases and in cheap hotels. He has been injured, cut from teams, blindly reassigned, and lowballed in contract negotiations. Through it all, he continues to pursue the NHL dream. It takes a very special type of human to accept the fate of a journeyman goaltender for this long, but with an unyielding faith and a loving family at his side, the pride of Charlottetown, Prince Edward Island carries that flag with pride and honor. He's also a great idol for young goalies; his career teaches you how one must be "comfortable being uncomfortable" in order to truly succeed at this level. You're not always going to get what you want, even if you worked hard enough to get it. And to think, if he didn't push past the fear of being less than an inch away from losing an eye while playing juniors in the QMJHL, his first NHL start with the Toronto Maple Leafs would've never happened.*

Valley: When we think about goaltending and the pressures you guys face on a nightly basis, we often use the term "Embracing the Grind" to explain it, because it's something everyone can relate to. With a pretty wild journey and pro career, what do you think of when we use that phrase? What is "the grind" to you?

MacIntyre: "It's just doing your job day in and day out, embracing the good with the bad. Thirteen years all in the minors; it can definitely be a grind sometimes. But I think truly embracing it is taking the hand that you were dealt and not laining while you're at it. I take a lot of pride in not complaining about any situation I'm in, whether it's a good one or a bad one."

Valley: If you're sitting at a table and across from you is 19-year-old Drew MacIntyre. What do you tell him?

MacIntyre: "Oh jeepers [laughing]. I tell him to relax. I tell him to relax and simplify. I'd get so mentally high and low, so I'd just tell him to breathe. Take a deep breath and relax and just let it happen. Like you guys say in *The Power Within*, it's about trusting the process. I put so much pressure on myself when I was younger, and I come from a small place, so there were a lot of people who were supporting me throughout my entire career. I remember I took a puck right into my cage during my draft year, and that was the reason why the CHL doesn't allow cat-eyes anymore. It was scary, but I remember my coach [Joe Canale] said, 'Buddy, this is the best thing to happen to you, because you put too much pressure on yourself.' I had started that season off poorly in the all-important draft year and I was ranked really high, so the pressure to turn things around was on. I was out for almost a month, so I got to relax and take a breath, but it took me a while to figure that lesson out."

Valley: I wanted to ask about that injury. The puck went right through your cage, right?

MacIntyre: "Right through it. Stephane Waite was my goalie coach at the time, and I remember it happened during a morning skate one day. I took the brunt of a slap shot right from the slot and Stephane said afterwards that it didn't go completely through and shatter, but it pushed the bars all the way back. He had to work pretty hard to pry the puck out of the cage."

Valley: It had to be a vicious shot if that's what initiated the rule change. What exactly happened to you?

MacIntyre: "They had to graft bone from my jaw and then insert two metal plates into my orbital bone, and I also broke my nose. But I got really lucky. If the puck had landed any higher, I would have lost my eye for sure."

Valley: So your coach told you this was the best thing to happen to you. Did it help?

MacIntyre: "Oh yeah. I had a good rest of the year. I was on a really poor team during my whole junior career, but I also had the chance to play all of the time. I also had Stephane as a goalie coach. It makes me giggle; people used to ask me all the time if I wish I were on a really good team, because I probably would've had a better chance to play for Team Canada or get drafted a little higher. But for my development and my path, it was great. I had Stephane and I always got a lot of shots."

Valley: So the one thing you tell young Drew MacIntyre is to chill out and relax. What do you tell him about the next 13 years and what to expect from all the highs and lows?

MacIntyre: "I'd tell him to expect everything. I mean, I've been in all kinds of situations. I've been in the ECHL struggling, I've been in the ECHL with a lot of success. I've been in the AHL struggling, and I've been in the AHL with a lot of success. I even got to play one game at the top, starting one game in the NHL. So you just have to expect everything. Anything you can think of is going to come at you. Don't get too high and don't get too low, just be thankful for what you have. Your career and your success isn't based on if you played in the NHL, so remember that there's a lot of other ways to be successful in pro hockey. I'm thankful that I've been playing in the minors for 13 years. I'm thankful for what I've been given, and I think it has all happened for a reason. My faith has had a lot to do with it, and I've had a good attitude about it all, so I don't complain about having success in the minors and still not really getting a chance in the NHL."

Valley: With 13 years in the minors, was there any time that sticks out as the absolute hardest time you've had? Did it ever get to the point that you didn't think you could fight through it anymore?

MacIntyre: "Yep. I mean, the year that I'm having right now has been tough. It just hasn't been fun. It's like you said about how some people just don't get it, you know? I'm in a situation with someone who just doesn't get it, and that's frustrating [laughing]. But my biggest one was when I went to the KHL. I broke my ankle, came back, and couldn't get a job. I was healthy and ready to go in early-December, but couldn't get a job anywhere in professional hockey. I started calling the East Coast, the Central League, but I had to wait a month and a half. Meanwhile, I was just living at home and practicing with a University team. I finally got a call to go to Reading in the the ECHL. I went to Reading for like a month and a half, and I was playing really well there. But goalies were dropping [getting injured] above me and I still wasn't getting any calls. It got to a point where I had my two daughters and my wife living in a hotel in Reading, Pennsylvania [laughing]. So I definitely had a few of those, 'Holy cow, what am I doing here?' moments. Luckily, I got a call from Toronto, and they gave me a really good opportunity. It went really well after that and I was able to re-establish myself."

Valley: So what got you through those times? When you're in that type of situation, what gave you the strength and fortitude to push forward?

MacIntyre: "For me, everything comes back to faith. That's my number one pillar; everything in my being really comes back to that. I understand that's not everybody, but it's definitely for me and my wife as well. She didn't sign up for 13 years of living in a different city almost every year, so she's been my rock. It's just amazing to see the support she gives me. Early in my career, it was all about making the NHL. If I didn't make the NHL, then I was a complete failure. So my wife and her faith made it easy to realize that I was going to be OK. If the NHL never comes, then I'm going to be okay."

Valley: Well, the NHL did come, and you had your first game in the NHL. Take me through that whole process.

MacIntyre: "I was up there for two or three weeks, and at the time, the Leafs were originally in the playoff hunt, but then they went on a big losing skid. So the whole thing was crazy, because I was having a really good year with the Marlies. I got called up when [Jonathan] Bernier was out with an injury and [James] Reimer had been having an up-and-down year. It was really frustrating at the time, because every day you think you're going to get your chance. I've been called up a few times for solid stints in Vancouver, Buffalo, and now Toronto. But for whatever reason, I just hadn't been able to get a start. Those teams just kept riding their guy. The whole knock against me my whole career, and I'd hear it every summer, was a lack of NHL experience. So that's been the most frustrating times and parts of my whole career; I just can't seem to get a chance while I'm up there to gain the experience I need. But it was really cool, because I was in Florida at the time, and we had mathematically been eliminated from the playoffs the night before. With only two games left in the season, they gave me the start in Florida. Rick St. Croix — he's a good friend of mine — told me I was going to play, so I had a day to think about it. It was just really cool. I remember during the National Anthem, I looked up and saw the banner that had the 2001 NHL Entry Draft logo on it, from when it was held in Florida. I kind of chuckled and smiled to myself during the anthem, because this start was in the building I got drafted in, and that was on my 18th birthday. And now 13 years later, or 12 and a half years later, whatever it was, I started my first game in the NHL. It was so cool. It was a fun experience for sure."

Valley: Were you nervous?

MacIntyre: "Yeah, I was nervous. I mean, I still get nervous. I just played last night and I was nervous, you know? I care about what I'm doing. I have a passion for it. I get nervous because I want to help my team win. So I was nervous at the time, but I was feeling really good about my game. The result wasn't great, we lost 4-1, but I had a good game and I faced 40-plus shots so it was a fun game to play. It would have been awesome to win, and even though there weren't a lot of people in the building — it wasn't the atmosphere that I expected for my first NHL start — it was a lot of fun and I am thankful for the experience."

Valley: So you've come to terms with maybe not having a full-time NHL career, and I say maybe, because you still never know. I've seen it happen to other guys. With that being said, what if all of a sudden you fast forward 20 years and you look back at your career. What are the best memories that came out of playing pro and junior hockey?

MacIntyre: "That's a good question, I'd have to think about it."

Valley: Or is it just actually playing that long and enjoying all the little things being with good teams?

MacIntyre: "I've been really close to winning some championships. I haven't won one yet, but I've been really close a few times, and those runs are a lot of fun to look back at. The playoffs is what you play for, and you get so close to the group of guys when you go through something like that, so those playoff runs are going to be something that I hope I never forget. Of course there's my games in the NHL, but really, it's just 13 years, and hopefully more coming, of just playing. If it ends tomorrow, I'm going to be totally okay, but I do love this game. I'm thankful that I get to do this for so long. I don't know what the ultimate memory will be, but I think it's just being able to do it as long as I have. I still look forward to practice, I like hanging out with the guys, I love everything. I'll always remember how fun it was to get that feeling of playing and being in control. I can forget the feelings when you struggle [laughing], but the feeling of being in control and knowing that they're not going to score is a great feeling."

Valley: What's the best piece of advice you ever received that you feel has helped you the most?

MacIntyre: "Oh man. I mean, I've played in so many different organizations. If I rattle off all the goalie coaches that I've had, it's an impressive list. I've had the best goalie coaches in the game. Most of them I didn't have full time, but I still had a chance to work with some of the best in the game. I've had so much good advice and I have a really good sports psychologist, which I think was one thing that saved me."

Valley: What happened exactly that led you to reach out to one?

MacIntyre: "I was hurt my entire first year as a pro, then I really struggled in my second year. I barely played; I was a backup to Joey MacDonald, who led the league in minutes played that year. I had a tough start and quickly realized that, if I wanted to make a career of this, I didn't have much time left. I was going into the last year of my deal when I met with the sports psychologist. I knew that I had to get a lot better, but I also knew that my attention to detail was keeping me in the game. I was also willing to work with a sports psychologist when I was 20 years old — I was able to listen to everybody and take it all in and process it all. Not everything's worked, but my attention to detail is what has kept me in it this long. I don't have more skill than all the other goalies I play with, but I battle, and I really want to get better. That's the thing; I couldn't tell you how often I hear the voice of my coach [Joe Canale] in my head from that meeting when I was 18. 'You've got to relax and enjoy the game.' I was 17 or 18 years old and I had all of that weight on my shoulders. I remember going into my draft year, I was on the ice *every* day that summer. I was possessed, like I *had* to be out there. But he told me, less is more. That's something I still strive to do. I've always worked hard, but you have to work in a controlled way. You have to work with a purpose."

Valley: It's also something where I think you're young and you don't quite understand what it really takes.

MacIntyre: "Absolutely. I had a lot of skill, but I was all over the place back then. There was no control in my game. I just had to learn that whenever I'm playing at my best, it's a simple game. I'm letting it come to me, and if needed, I can still make the odd two-pad stack. Nowadays my technique is just simple, and when it's simple, that's when I'm playing at my best."

Valley: What about emotional control? I even remember playing against you in the ECHL and you've always been a competitive guy. But over the course of 13 years, what have you learned about emotional control? How does your mind work when things are not going your way?

MacIntyre: "One time I hit a guy in front of the net, because I didn't like the way he was screening me. I just laid into him. After the game, I remember Stephane Waite taught me a lesson. 'Why do that?' he asked. 'Why waste your energy on that?' They had scored on the play and I was hitting the guy, and I didn't even attempt to track the puck. So over the past couple of years, I've always kept Roger Federer in mind. The way that he plays is how I want to play the game. You can never tell if Federer is up or down in a game. You watch other tennis players, and you can 100-percent tell when they're starting to lose emotional control. They're hitting their racket, they're looking at their coach sitting in the boxes, and they're getting so rattled. But Federer is so 'ho-hum' out there. If he's losing, he's not hard on himself. Obviously I haven't accomplished this to Federer's degree, but it's what I strive to be like. I want to be competitive, but in a controlled way. I take a lot of pride in accomplishing that."

Valley: Once you learned how to better control your emotions before and during the game, did you find that it helped manage your energy? When you were young, did you drain yourself?

MacIntyre: "Totally. At the start of my career, I think that was the ultimate reason why I called the sports psychologist. I worked really hard to get into great shape, but I'd be so tired! I could practice all day, but in a game, I was so mentally drained. That was the one thing I couldn't figure out. I'd be so drained from thinking about the game all day. I was so up, and then the crash would come. When you're watching Federer, it looks like he's not even breaking a sweat. I can always tell when I'm a little rattled by the amount I'm sweating. If I have to take my shirt off after the first period, I know I need to calm down. I sweat more when I'm rattled."

Valley: How do you get yourself to calm down?

MacIntyre: "I use a few breathing techniques. Every intermission for about two minutes, I pull my hat down over my head and breathe in and out for long periods, and at the same time I do a little visualization. I've done it every intermission for a long, long time, so that gets me to breathe better, calm down, and be more in the moment."

Valley: Anyone who watches you in warmups sees that little meditation ritual you do at the red line. That's gone on for how long and what purpose does that serve?

MacIntyre: "For my entire career. I started that in Toledo in the Coast [ECHL] and those are really the only two times I do it. I pray at the end of warmups for about a minute and just focus on my breathing. It's like I read in *The Power Within* about detaching yourself. I just want to breathe with more focus and control so that I am centered. So I'm there. When you're in warmups, it's almost like you can get too amped up. The breathing gets you centered in the moment."

Valley: I like studying a little bit about the aura we portray on others. If guys see that you're calm, it totally changes the way that they start playing the game as well. We learn that as we get older.

MacIntyre: "I never want to be the type of goalie that the other team points at as being able to chirp or easily get off his game. I've heard that about a lot of goalies, and I've always thought I'd hate to be one of those guys. Whenever I have a playoff series against somebody, they don't really ever try to talk to me much, because they know it never does anything. I could care less what you say to me during a game. It doesn't bother me and I'm not going to mouth off to you. That's not me."

Valley: One thing that's really tough for goalies is that we have very little control in a game where we *have* to play as controlled as possible. It's tough, because we can prepare and feel as ready as we want, but at the end of the day, it's a team game and things happen in front of you, things that you don't always have control over. When you're younger, you try to control everything, and that actually starts to work against you. When you get older, you actually learn to just let go, and then things actually become more controlled. The more you let go, the easier it becomes. Have you noticed the same thing after 13 years of embracing the grind?

MacIntyre: "One hundred percent. I say that to myself a lot. The past few years in Charlotte, especially last year, was the first time in a long time that I was on a weak team. I've been really lucky to be on some of the best AHL organizations, but in my final year with Carolina, we were near the bottom all year and I really, really had to learn it. I've always had to learn it, but the past two years, I've had to remind myself all the time to completely detach myself from the result. I always say '...next shot...' to myself. I haven't won as much lately as I have in the past, so I've had to remind myself that I can't control how much my team is going to score. I've had to appreciate a different definition of a good night or a successful game."

Valley: Are you able to leave it at the rink after a good day or bad day?

MacIntyre: "Yeah, I am. I have two daughters and a wife, so I have to. I don't want to be that dad. I'm in the middle of a tough season right now; I've taken the game home with me and I've been a little grumpy at times. So hockey is very important to me, but it's not my number one. I'm not going to let it ruin the time I spend with my family."

Valley: Would you do it again? If you had to do it all over again, would you? And what would you do differently?

MacIntyre: "One hundred percent, I'd do it again. Absolutely. I have buddies back home that don't care I'm not in the NHL. They're just proud I was able to make a career out of it. They follow me and support me like they're going through it themselves, so it's really cool to be able to do that and have their support. I've been able to do what I love for this long — are you kidding me? Of course I'd do it again. In a heartbeat. What would I do different? I don't know. I'm a true believer that things happen for a reason. Some of the biggest lessons I've learned in life have been through hockey. I've learned so many lessons about patience. I've been in crappy situations where I've wanted things to change right away. I wanted a solution right away, even if ending that situation meant getting traded or signing with a new team. But you have to trust the process. A lot of it has to do with my faith, but some of the greatest lessons I've learned are not just about hockey, but key life lessons that I'll eventually teach my two girls."

Chapter 16
TIME, TREASURES, TALENTS

"Only a man who knows what it is like to be defeated can reach down to the bottom of his soul and come up with the extra ounce of power it takes to win when the match is even." - Muhammad Ali

Before reading on, take a quick moment to ponder the following question: What's one thing all goaltenders carry with them at all times, both on and off the ice?

If you said an extra stick or a spare set of skate laces, you're certainly not wrong. But that's not quite the answer we're looking for here. Think a little more outside the box.

If you said confidence, you're on the right track, but the answer we're looking for is quite simple. The one thing you always carry with you as a goalie is your identity. As the last line of defense, you're also responsible for a significant portion of a team's identity.

How many times have you struggled early in a game, only to witness your teammates somehow absorb those same struggles? You make a few bad reads or give up a few bad rebounds and all of a sudden they can't make tape-to-tape passes or get out of their own end. It's a bit eerie, yet it happens all the time, thus proving you have some type of resounding impact on the identity of a team. It happens as much off the ice as it does on the ice.

Your identity as a goaltender and a person is always changing. It's molded by your beliefs, your attitude, your personality, and who you choose to be around. It can also be defined as the combination of three key elements working side-by-side to shape your fate:

Time, treasures, and talents.

Time is a valuable thing; you only have a finite amount of it. Therefore, the time you commit to playing the game of hockey carries a very meaningful tone. You choose to do this; it is your calling, your passion, and a big part of your identity. This leads to many important decisions regarding your desires and dreams, for you have to be smart with the little time you have on this earth.

Treasures also carry great value; the things and experiences you acquire and accumulate over time act as a credence for where you're going and what you want to achieve. Treasures are not only things, but the memories, friendships, and opportunities you hold closest to your hearts.

Talents, however, might be the most valuable part of your identity. Talents, both genetic and trained, are gifts. If you're born with a talent for goaltending, you must appreciate that it was a special combination of your parents and upbringing. If you developed the skill over time all on your own, then you must appreciate the hard work you've put in to create it.

Now take all three elements — your time, treasures, and talents — and offer them up. Sacrifice them all for the greater good of your teammates, family, loved ones, and those who look up to you. Realize that all three things are gifts that are meant to be shared, gifts that can make this world a better place, and gifts that can lift the spirit of others.

Do this, and you'll never fail at the game of hockey or life. For your time will never be wasted, your treasures will never be forgotten, and your talents will never go unnoticed.

Chapter 17
FRED BRATHWAITE

Introduction: *If you include his junior hockey career with the OHL's Oshawa Generals and his time spent with Adler Mannheim in Germany's top pro league (DEL), Freddy Brathwaite played at some of the highest levels imaginable for over 20 years. During those two decades, his personal and professional grinds were unimaginable to most of us. Not only was he one of the first men of color to stop pucks in the NHL, but he was also one of the smallest. With a 254-game NHL career under his belt, Brathwaite now carries the burden of being Hockey Canada's top goaltending consultant. On the road for what seems like an endless stretch of flights, bus rides, and phone calls, Freddy travels from province to province working with Canada's top young goaltenders. It's no secret he has one of the most under-appreciated gigs in hockey, but that won't stop him from pursuing his latest dream — to be an NHL goalie coach. We feel it's only a matter of time until it happens, and until then, he remains a goaltending icon, a role model, and a true reflection of what the grind is all about.*

Valley: Let's dive right in with a tough one. When I ask you what the phrase "Embracing the Grind" means, what's the first thing that comes to mind regarding your career?

Brathwaite: "For one thing, I obviously had some issues due to my size. Only being five-foot-seven, people said there was no way I would be able to play in the NHL. And while I don't like to use this as an excuse, the color thing was a small issue, too. So for me, every day, I just wanted to try and prove people wrong, and that's what motivated me to keep getting better. Growing up, my favorite goalies were Darren Pang and Grant Fuhr, which of course ended up being a small guy and a black guy [laughing]. Pang grew up in Ottawa right near my neighborhood and we went to the same high school, but not at the same time. We also played in the same minor hockey organization with the Nepean Raiders, so growing up and watching him make it [to the NHL] was a big thing for me. Then seeing someone like Grant Fuhr do what he did was great motivation as well. He wasn't *the* first, but one of the first goalies to break the color barrier."

Valley: You had some great mentors and idolized some great goalies when you were growing up, which we all need when we're working towards a pro hockey career. But what about your actual personality? What is it about Freddy Brathwaite that made him so mentally tough and physically durable for all those years?

Brathwaite: "A big thing for me was that I really enjoyed playing the game. I loved going to the rink. I enjoyed practicing and trying to get better, and like I said earlier, I loved trying to prove people wrong by just going out there and showing them I could do it. I did have some issues, though. I mean, I had a pretty good junior career and played in two junior All-Star games, but all my backup partners would get drafted, not me. That all happened before I got my opportunity in Edmonton, when a guy named Ted Green gave me a chance to play with Bill Ranford."

Valley: So this guy offered you a tryout?

Brathwaite: "Well, at the time, I went to their development camp as a walk-on and then got invited back to their main camp. A couple of things worked out in my favor there. A goalie named Wayne Cowley, who had won the Calder Cup the year before, didn't have a good camp. They also had a second-year pro named Andrew Verner, but all of a sudden I was backing up Ranford as a 21-year-old. After playing three years in Edmonton, I started to think that I was actually pretty good. But I eventually realized that I didn't work as hard as I probably should have and found myself back in the minors for the next two years. One year was with Vincent Riendeau and then the other was with Johan Hedberg. The way my contract worked in the IHL was strange; all of a sudden I was making too much money. It got to the point where the IHL started getting more guys from the NHL, and that's when I lost my job again. From there I ended up going to play with the National team, made $18,000 that year, went to the Spengler Cup, and won it all. I came back to Ottawa and got a call from my agent and he said, 'Freddy, they want you to go down and play in St. John's.' I was obviously pretty excited about that, so I said, 'Yeah I'll go, but my equipment's in Calgary.' So I ended up going to Calgary to practice with the Flames. The next night they informed me that they didn't have a goalie, so I would be starting against Dallas. Going into the game, Dallas had won eight in a row and Calgary had lost eight in a row, but we ended up beating them 2-0, which really re-energized my whole career."

Valley: That's a crazy twist and a cool story. Where were you slated to be on Calgary's depth chart at the time?

Brathwaite: "I was probably seventh or eighth."

Valley: And then all of a sudden you got a chance.

Brathwaite: "Yeah, I got my chance and I took it. The thing I reflect about right now is how I really had nothing to lose. I just went out there and played. They didn't have any other goalies available, so I remember going out there and saying, 'You know what Freddy? This is an opportunity. Just try to run with it. Have fun. Just have fun.' Not too many people get second chances; I got one and told myself to make the most of it. In Calgary, I also realized that I had to work way harder to stay in the league. It wasn't just about being a good guy in the locker room."

Valley: Yeah, you've always been known as a great guy. We love having you in Madison.

Brathwaite: "Well luckily I was finally starting to figure the rest of it out, too. I ended up sticking around and staying in Calgary for the entire year. My roommate at the time, Tyler Moss, got sent down, [J.S.] Giguere was still in the minors, and I ended up working harder. But I was enjoying it too. I really enjoyed just getting to know the guys and getting that opportunity to play. Then all of a sudden I got traded to St. Louis."

Valley: That came out of left field and your role changed a little bit. Who were you playing with in St. Louis?

Brathwaite: "I started off behind Brent Johnson, and then Tom Barrasso came. From there, I actually got released right at the Trade Deadline, because they brought in Chris Osgood at the last minute."

Valley: We ask this question to each guy in the book, and I think because you got hit with another bad break, now is a good time to ask. If you were sitting at a table right now and across from you was a 21-year-old Freddy Brathwaite, what would you tell him?

Brathwaite: "I would tell him to learn how to work every day. Enjoy the moment, but work every day like it's your last day. That's something I didn't do when I was 21. I might have enjoyed it too much, but didn't realize how hard it was to stay in the league or what it took to keep working. I was lucky enough to play with Ranford when he was still one of the best goalies in the league, and I played with Curtis Joseph when he was one of the best. I even played with Mike Vernon and Fuhr, so I was lucky enough to be around some guys that really enjoyed it, but also worked extremely hard. Ranford did not want to get scored on, ever. Guys would shoot from the corner and he would dive back to make saves and do all kinds of stuff to keep the puck out. The other thing I would tell my younger self is to take in everything that everyone is telling you. Today we have so many resources and ways to get better. That would have been awesome for me back then, because I wanted to get better, but I didn't have too many resources available. We didn't really have the internet, the video analysis, or full-time goalie coaches back then. The game is a little different now than it was when we were playing."

Valley: We were on an island by ourselves.

Brathwaite: "We were! We really were. There wasn't a lot of involvement in the game, especially in goaltending, back then."

Valley: If you look back at that now, was getting dropped by St. Louis one of the most frustrating points in your career? Were you at a point where you thought it was over?

Brathwaite: "Yeah, there were a couple of those times. I mean, not getting drafted was frustrating. At the time, I was thinking to myself, 'You know what? You better figure out what else you're going to do with your life.' Very seldom did people make it as a walk-on, but I thought I was playing pretty well when I was breaking through with Edmonton. I still couldn't find a job, though. I signed in Las Vegas for $27,000 and thought it was pretty much over at that point. Then I went to St. Louis, but they got Chris Osgood at the Trade Deadline. When they came to me and said, 'Fred, we don't need you anymore,' I thought my career was done. I thought I had a good little run, but my time in the NHL was over. Then I suddenly got an opportunity from Columbus, and leading up to that I can remember thinking, 'Jeez, if I ever get one more chance, for sure I'm going to work harder and do whatever I have to do to stay in the league.' I went to Columbus and *still* didn't work as hard as I could have, so obviously I didn't play that well, either. That was the most frustrating part of my career; I tried to prepare myself way better than I actually showed, and I just didn't play well. Maybe I was just thinking too much. I don't know."

Valley: What got you through those days? Those times when you thought it was close to being over — what pushed you through that and what kept you going?

Brathwaite: "My brother. He's had a huge influence on me. He would just say, 'Hey you know what, if you get an opportunity, embrace it. You don't want to work at the shopping mall.' So he knew that I loved the game and that I didn't know what I was going to do after that. I will always remember having those talks with my brother. He'd say, 'Fred, yeah it has been a good ride, but you can still do more. If you get that opportunity, really try to run with it.' So I think the biggest thing was the positive influence from my brother. Then of course my parents and some close friends. The other thing that was really important for me was just the pure love of the game."

Valley: Those bad breaks, like getting traded or being waived, were all external factors. Internally, was there ever a point where, just in your own mind, you decided that you didn't want to do this anymore? Or did you just love the game that much?

Brathwaite: "You know what? I just loved the game too much. I was someone who would go to the rink and enjoy being around the guys far too much. I don't think there was ever a time where I thought I was totally done, even when I signed with

Atlanta and they signed Hedberg at the same time. When that happened, the next thing I know, I was back in the minors. And you know what? I went down there, because you just never know what's going to happen. So I never got to the point where I hated the game and didn't want to do it anymore. In fact, it wasn't until my last professional year, when we lost in the finals over in Germany, that I probably knew it was over. I was 39 years old at the time. That's when I sat back and realized it was finally over."

Valley: You talked about your brother earlier, but what about your parents? Were they supportive throughout the process? How was your relationship with them?

Brathwaite: "Yeah, they were very supportive. For one thing, my mom never watched me play live. She was always too worried and too scared that I was going to get hurt. Even when I was 39 and nearing retirement, she still didn't watch me play live. She came to Germany during my last year and saw me play two games, and that was it. She and my dad were always supportive. Obviously my dad wanted to see me do well, but he was the voice of reasoning, too. On some days I had to be pretty hard on myself, but he helped me to be realistic and kept me grounded. He would say 'Don't worry about it, tomorrow's another day,' and stuff like that. My parents grew up in Barbados, but they didn't know the sport that well. They were more supportive to me more as a person than a goaltender."

Valley: If you look back at your pro career now, what would you say was the biggest grind of being a pro goalie?

Brathwaite: "The hardest thing for me was being consistent."

Valley: Why is it so hard to be consistent?

Brathwaite: "That's a good question. As a goaltender, you can't just work hard to play well. You can't look at the puck harder. You can't have quicker recoveries and just hope you stop the puck more. Obviously you try and get into that rhythm, but I think even though everyone's different, they still over-think too much about what they did the day before or what has happened in the past, and that's exactly why they can't stay in that rhythm."

Valley: I agree with you 100-percent that you can't try harder. As a skater, you can go out and hit someone or skate harder. But as a goalie, there are so many things that aren't in your control. There's a luck factor that comes into all this and interferes with your rhythm as well; how good your team is, how prepared they are. So I agree that there are things you can't control, and that's what makes it so hard to be consistent.

Brathwaite: "You can start a game with a great warmup and you're feeling good, but then the first shot goes off your defenseman's foot and in, and all of a sudden you're down 1-0. Meanwhile, the other goalie has nothing go right in the warmup, has the first shot hit two posts and bounce out, and now somehow that's the bounce he needed to get him going. It could have gone either way. It's a funny game."

Valley: Now you're traveling all over North America and seeing this on a daily basis with Canada's top junior goaltenders. Based off your experiences as a player, how do you tell these kids to handle this type of situation emotionally?

Brathwaite: "I tell them how your body language is a huge thing. The vibe you give off to your teammates and others is a big thing. I want to be there and watch these kids when they get scored on, because I want to see their body language, I want to see how their teammates react to them, and I want to see how the goalie responds after that."

Valley: How did you learn this lesson for yourself at the pro level?

Brathwaite: "That's something I learned from being with Fuhr. I've told you this story before, but he used to drink Mountain Dew on the bench. Well, one game I let in a goal from the other blue line, and I mean it was a really bad goal. At the next TV timeout, I skate to the bench, he hands me one of those green Gatorade water bottles, and I spray it all over my face thinking it's water. But it was Mountain Dew! I just looked at him and he started laughing at me and said, 'Freddy, there's nothing you can do about it. Just go back out there and keep playing!' What's happened in the past has happened in the past. Obviously you're sad or mad or whatever, but you can't allow the other team to know it. So how do you control those emotions? I think you've got to start and finish by having a really short memory."

Valley: It's probably part of your DNA after your upbringing, and that's why I asked about your parents and brother. "Embracing the Grind" is just who you are as a person. You almost have to learn how to not care. It's like when you would see Timmy Thomas just smiling under his mask after giving up some goals. The aura and the body language that you send out actually does influence the game in certain ways.

Brathwaite: "Benoit Groulx, who is coaching at Gatineau this season, coached us at the World Juniors and told this story. He said after last year's Super Bowl, he stayed up until three or four in the morning reading all of the different articles. He read one on how a Broncos player knew they had shut down Cam Newton when his body language started changing. Shortly after that, he started yapping at the refs, and at that moment, they knew they were in his head. It's so true, right? If I saw a goalie that gets bumped into and gets beat as a result, and he's huffing and puffing and pointing his stick, I'd be telling the coach to put guys in front of him, because he's already rattled. So yeah, I think a huge part of it is the person themselves and their discipline."

Valley: It almost seems like the best way to deal with the grind as a goalie is not by being an oak tree that tries to stand there and always fight against the elements, but more like a willow tree, just bending and swaying in all directions. Like your story with Fuhr, you almost have to laugh at yourself and just go with it.

Brathwaite: "There's too many things that can happen in a game that you can't control, but there are some big things you can control, and that's your body language and the way you prepare for a game. All these silly little things that you can't control — if you let them take over your game when it goes awry, it's way tougher to embrace the grind."

Valley: How about when you're in a slump? How do guys push themselves through that grind? Is it luck or is it hard work?

Brathwaite: "I think it's a combination of everything. It's hard work, and like we've talked about before, it's also repetition, because you're trying to get guys feeling good by putting them in drills where they can get their confidence back in practice. It's a bit mental as well. There has to be a mental skill of understanding the game and knowing that things aren't always going to happen the way you expect. You can't let that frustration or disappointment take over."

Valley: Knowing that some of the kids reading this book are 16 or 17 years old, and knowing that some of the goalies you're scouting could go through 20 years of the pro-level grind, what's one thing you want readers to know about the journey?

Brathwaite: "Never give up on your dream, no matter what it may be. Never get too high, never get too low. Just keep pushing and working to be the best version of yourself every single day."

Chapter 18

Be Gritty and Genuine

"The best way out is always through." - Robert Frost

Goaltending is a humbling journey. The more you play the position and the more minutes you log in the crease, the more you realize how little you can actually control. You also learn over time that having talent is only half the battle.

The other half? Being genuine.

Having success on that side of the battle doesn't solely depend on being even-keeled and having complete emotional control 24-7. It's also about having the grit needed to embrace the grind and having the genuine spirit needed to always give 110-percent. To be genuine is to be intimately in tune with who you are and what you truly want to accomplish in life.

Gritty and genuine goaltenders have an ability to cope with the things they can't control. They know that they are stuck with the unfairness and unwarranted failures of their past, and bound to the fate and follies of their future as well. Whether the outcome is a dream come true or a total nightmare, the truly elite goalies have a genuine appreciation and love for the daily battle.

The "grind" doesn't scare them or cause them to suddenly live in fear. In fact, it doesn't even register as having a negative impact on anything in their lives. They just trudge through it all with incredible resolve and a willingness to bend, flow, and roll with the punches. Whatever it takes, it's getting done, whether they get through it unharmed or not.

Having a genuine or authentic personality is no longer a buzzword for pop sports psychology, either. Empirical research in the field of authenticity is clearly still evolving, but it does suggest that genuine people have a more positive outlook and "vibe" in their social circles and daily lives. As a result, it can lead these people to more inner confidence and better body language, two things that every goaltender needs.

Grit can have many definitions, but its link to being genuine is found in the ability to embrace every obstacle imaginable.

Are you able to suck it up when a coach that doesn't like your style benches you for no reason? Do you have the discipline to wake up at 4:30 in the morning five days a week to do a bag skate and a private lesson before school for an entire season?

If you answered yes to these questions, then you're pretty gritty.

Are you willing to pursue these dreams no matter the cost, even if it ultimately costs you love? Do you feel connected with your spirit and environment when you're playing? Is goaltending in your blood and a part of you until the day you die? Are you willing to leave behind everyone you know and love just to pursue the dream of college or junior hockey?

If you answered yes to these questions, then you're pretty genuine.

No matter how bad you want it or how genuine you are in pursuing it, developing the grit necessary to accomplish the goal takes plenty of pain and sacrifice. So push forward and continue to fight the storms, the wind, and the thunder. Navigate through the tumultuous seas and all of life's adversities and aim straight for the shores of success you're destined to discover!

Chapter 19

JOHAN HEDBERG

Introduction: *Selected 218th overall in the 1994 NHL Draft by the Philadelphia Flyers, Johan Hedberg was an afterthought for many in the organization. When scouts forced him to make the Swedish National Team before receiving a tryout, Hedberg put his nose to the grindstone and got it done. He kept his side of the bargain, only to find the Flyers would fail to keep theirs. But that didn't stop him from crossing the sea and pursuing his NHL dream. Roaming all over North America and playing for all types of wild creatures like the Baton Rouge Kingfish, the Detroit Vipers, the Manitoba Moose, and the Kentucky Thoroughblades, Hedberg finally got his chance when the Pittsburgh Penguins came calling late in the 2000-01 season. Donning his iconic "Moose" mask, he knocked out two legendary goalie giants in Godzilla (Olaf Kolzig) and the Dominator (Dominik Hasek) in order to reach the Eastern Conference Finals. Twelve NHL seasons and 373 total games later, Hedberg's playing career ended with admirable service for the New Jersey Devils. He transitioned into goalie and assistant coaching with the San Jose Sharks seamlessly, bringing life full-circle; he was actually buried in San Jose's depth chart when that magical trade to Pittsburgh transpired. It's just more proof that embracing the grind can result in becoming a true diamond in the rough.*

Goldman: If you were to reflect back on your NHL career, what does the book title "Embracing the Grind" mean to you? How would you define it?

Hedberg: "To me, 'The Grind' is when you do things over and over and over again. Things that you believe in, or things that you want to do to become better. From the first day of summer workouts through the grind of an entire season, the goal is to become a better goaltender. I would probably describe that as my personal definition of it. Playing an entire season can be a real grind, but I think it's something really personal, too. It's something that you go through in your life and playing career where you learn, gain experience, and grow from those moments."

Goldman: Could you reflect on that personal grind? Was there a certain point in your career where you were really feeling it emotionally?

Hedberg: "It was when I came over [from Sweden]. I got drafted late by Philadelphia when I was 21 and was extremely excited, because the only thing I ever dreamed of was to get a chance to play in the NHL. I didn't have an agent and I didn't know anything about the process, so I was really naive about it. The only person I talked to was their Swedish scout, Inge Hammarstrom. He said, 'You know what? We like you, but we want you to play for the Swedish National Team before we'll be interested in your services.' So when I made the National Team, I asked, 'Well what about now?' [pause] 'No, now we need you to be the *starter* on the National Team," he said. But every time the World Championships came around, Tommy Soderstrom would come home and be the starter. I felt like that was out of my hands, so I ended up signing a deal with the Detroit Vipers in the IHL. They were an independent team at the time, but I felt like I had to come over [to North America] and prove to them on their turf that I could do it. I think that's a little description of when I was grinding it out and trying to achieve my goals. I had a good situation in Sweden — I was playing well for my home team and was on the National team. But that's not what the ultimate goal was. I wanted to take my grind over here and prove it to Inge and the hockey world that I could do it."

Goldman: I remember reading about that a few years ago. The Flyers told you to make the National Team, you made it, but they never actually offered you the camp invite!

Hedberg: "True, I never got invited."

Goldman: How did that make you feel? Mentally, I couldn't imagine working so hard to attain that goal and then still not get the opportunity you were supposed to get.

Hedberg: "In that case, I knew it was not in my hands. I felt like it wouldn't matter how good I played at home. When push comes to shove, for them, it was about me being the starter on the National team — it was the deciding factor. But I knew a guy was coming back over from North America and would automatically be named the starter, so I couldn't control my own destiny. I needed to do something where I could, and that's when I felt like the only thing I could do to make this work was to come to North America, take charge of my situation, and just do it."

Goldman: You mentioned that you didn't have any real guidance or anyone to lean on. How tough was that for you to push through? All of the questions and all of that not knowing if it would pan out. How did that feel?

Hedberg: "When I finally went to North America, I got an agent. But the first two years after being drafted, I never had one. Maybe if I did, he would've helped me and told me what I was supposed to do to get that invite [laughing]. I just went about my business and tried to be so good that they had to bring me over. After I got an agent, we went over all my choices and it was a last-minute resort to approach the Vipers for an opportunity. At that time, I was almost done. My next one-way ticket back [to Sweden] was going to be it. They signed another goalie and the opportunity I had to play a lot over here went away, but signing with the Vipers ended up being a good situation. They traded me in the spring, I learned a lot from that, and it kick-started my NHL journey."

Goldman: Mike said he had a pretty cool experience with you. He said you guys were hanging out after a game in Houston one night, and before you joined the Penguins, you were pretty open with him about your concerns over getting a legit shot to play in the NHL, getting that big chance. Then he said you were suddenly traded to Pittsburgh a few days later. Can you talk a little bit about what happened before you got that big chance?

Hedberg: "The first time I met Mike, I actually had no idea he spoke Swedish. It totally caught me off guard! But at that time, I was playing in Manitoba with Ken Wregget and having a good year, so things were going pretty well. But I was 27 years old at the time, so I didn't think I was ever going to get a chance to play in the NHL. It seemed to be getting further and further away. I knew the depth chart in San Jose went Mike Vernon, Steve Shields, Evgeni Nabokov, Miikka Kiprusoff, and then myself, so I knew I was way far down. The next year, Vernon retired and they signed Vesa Toskala, and so once again I felt like there was just no chance of breaking through."

Goldman: So basically you were in your darkest time just before you saw the bright light of a sudden trade to the Penguins.

Hedberg: "I remember we were playing in Cincinnati one night and we lost a big game, 7-1. We had a shitty outing; Wregget started and I mopped up. After the game, it was one of those nights where I was stressing a lot and starting to realize that my dream was never going to come true. I called my wife from the back of the restaurant that night, and like I did with Mike, I openly contemplated turning the page. I thought, maybe it's just not meant to be. [pause] 'Let's talk when we get home,' she said. 'Maybe you can play in Switzerland or something like that!' So we take a plane back home to Winnipeg that same night, because the Trade Deadline was the very next day. I was standing there with my wife after getting off the plane, and I was still thinking and talking about giving up and doing something else. But she said, 'No, no, just keep holding on. Good things are going to happen. Who knows, maybe you'll get traded tomorrow. I saw your GM over there on the phone, maybe you just got traded.' I just started laughing and treated it like yeah, right, whatever. Then we take the escalator upstairs and right around the corner is the GM and the head coach. When they saw me, they started waving me over. They wanted to talk, so I walk over to them. [pause] 'Well Johan, we just got off the phone with San Jose and they want you to call them.' As he was saying this, I figured I was just getting called up. Sure enough, my wife comes walking up beside me saying, 'What's going on, what's going on?!' I peeled away to call San Jose right away, and they just told me straight up, 'We think your dream just came true. We've traded you to Pittsburgh.' [pause] Then I said, 'What?! Pittsburgh? What am I going to do there?' I knew they were looking for a goalie, but they were talking big names, someone who could get them deep into the playoffs. So I asked, 'Am I reporting to Wilkes-Barre?' 'No, no,' they said. 'No, Johan, you're going there to play.' [pause] 'Are you serious? I'm going to Pittsburgh to play?!' That's how it all happened. It was so sudden."

Goldman: That's so amazing! That's such a perfect story to share with readers. It shows them first-hand how goalies can experience life at its worst right before it does a complete flip, and now suddenly your life as a goalie is exactly what you always wanted.

Hedberg: "The very next day, I called my brother right away [laughing]. He's like my biggest supporter and he has followed my career very closely. I told my wife I had to prank him, so I called him at his home in Sweden. Right away, he says, 'What were you guys doing last night? What's going on over there? You can't drop the ball like that, losing 7-1 to Cincinnati! That's not good enough.' So I stayed serious and said, 'Yeah, I know it wasn't. You know what, though? It's tough to say this, but to be honest Anders, I don't really give a crap anymore.' So he just totally blows up, 'What do you mean!? You can't give up! You can't give up! No!' So I cut him off and said, 'Guess what, I have to tell you something. I've just been traded.' He went nuts. 'What?! Where?! When?!' Then I cut him off again and said, 'Sorry, I can't hear you over here! It's breaking up! Your phone sucks! I gotta go!' [pause] 'Shut the hell up, Johan!! Tell me where you're going! What's happening?!' I waited a moment and then said, 'Dude, I got traded to Pittsburgh. I'm going there to play!' He's so blown away at this point, and that was it. I'm home just long enough to pack my bags, and the next morning I flew to Pittsburgh and got my start a couple of days later down in Florida. The whole thing was a dream come true. I've never been so excited and never been so positive and so charged up. It was an amazing experience."

Goldman: That's unreal! But wait, man. I have to know something. What the hell did you say to your wife after she predicted your trade to Pittsburgh?! That is borderline eerie but totally amazing [laughing].

Hedberg: "To be honest, I can't really remember. I just remember getting in the car with her and I just screamed, 'Aah! This is unbelievable!' 'I told you!' she said. 'Yeah, but how?!'"

Goldman: Wow. Pretty speechless.

Hedberg: "She never cared too much about hockey or anything like that, but obviously she was more interested in those early days. She wanted to push on, to see what the next chapter was going to bring into our lives. So she kept a pretty good pace with me during that period leading up to time right before the Trade Deadline."

Goldman: For you personally, what was the biggest lesson that came out of that crazy experience?

Hedberg: "I was never told that my play had anything to do with being traded while in the minors with Manitoba. But when I came to Pittsburgh, I was told later by a scout that he had been keeping a close eye on me for a long time and had watched me a lot of times. That brought me back to another lesson I learned my first year in North America. One night, I went out to dinner with Brent Fedyk, who used to play in the NHL, but was in the minors at the time. We all ordered food and then he ordered water, but everyone else was drinking wine. 'You don't want any wine?' I asked. 'No, no thanks. I'm fine,' he said. So you know what his lesson was to me? He said, 'The way I see it, Johan, it's that you never know. You never know who's going to be watching. You never know who's going to be up there. I need to make sure that I have the best game every chance I get, because you just never know. If I was in here drinking a lot of wine and beer, I may not give myself the best opportunity to get back up there [the NHL].' I thought it was a pretty cool thing for him to say, so I took it to heart and I've kept it that way. You always learn things about yourself that you can use down the road, and I learned from that one."

Goldman: From all the pro guys I've talked to over the years, it almost seems like a necessity. It's like you have to reach your breaking point before you can sustain success for more than a few games. Everyone has a different threshold, and pushing that limit is a big key to embracing the grind. Do you think in those moments leading up to the trade that you were experiencing a 'breaking point' in your career?

Hedberg: "Yes, for sure. I probably wouldn't have given up completely, but I was already 27 at the time. To get a chance that late in your career wasn't that common, so I really thought it just wasn't going to happen; there were just way too many guys ahead of me on this team. But San Jose was great about it. They always said, 'You know what, we know you see the depth chart and think this or that, but our philosophy is that we want you to play, and we want you to play in the NHL. If it's with us, that's great. If not, we want to find a place where you can play.' They were so awesome with me and my situation. We also had Warren Strelow, who was just a phenomenal goalie coach. I would have never played in the NHL if I hadn't met him and had the chance to work with him. He taught me how to be more consistent, how to develop a better understanding of my own game, how to prepare every day, and how to keep the little things going smooth all the time. The weeks he would come out and work with me and Kiprusoff, I didn't even care if I played in the games — it was so good to get the practice time with him."

Goldman: I wish I had a chance to meet him. I can remember watching CBC air a special on him and his influence on Evgeni Nabokov. Warren is an icon to me and a lot of my friends, because we're part of the new goalie development program coming out for USA Hockey, and being a part of the Strelow program for the past few years has been a dream come true. This is a bit of a selfish question, but was there an inspirational quote or phrase that he had that taught you about embracing the grind? Anything he taught you that you can remember about coping with the stress and pressure of being a pro goalie?

Hedberg: "You know what? Because I was always a hard worker — a hard worker on the ice and a hard worker off the ice — he always told me, 'What goes around comes around.' But at the time, I never got it. I just didn't have a good read on all of these different sayings in the English language [laughing]. So I was like, alright, whatever, because I just never knew what he meant. But I finally understood the meaning of that phrase the moment I got traded. I was like, 'Huh. That's what he meant. That's exactly it!' If you keep doing the right things, keep working the right way, and do what you are supposed to do to prepare, then good things will happen. What goes around comes around. You get what you deserve. All of these things are so truc. It's easy to give up. But if you stick with a dream, you keep doing it no matter what, and you keep going. You don't give up — things will come around. His message became so clear to me when I got traded to Pittsburgh and got a chance to play in the NHL. So 'What goes around comes around' has been my mantra for most of my career. I always tried to treat people with respect, to be a good person, to work as hard as I can, and to be as prepared as I could. It helped me gain confidence that things would go well. I think it's just our nature that you want to be a good human being, but it's also a great reminder, just to have something to hang your hat on. This is why I'm doing something. I believe in it. I'm going to do it. I would say that's probably one of the biggest and most important lessons I learned in my career. And it was from Warren Strelow."

Goldman: So after this crazy trade to the Penguins, everyone starts to know your name and story during that unreal Stanley Cup run in 2001. Can you reflect on that a little bit? What about your time in San Jose's system and training with Warren really prepared you to face that playoff grind in Pittsburgh?

Hedberg: "Oh, it was a lot of things. One of them was the technical game I learned from Warren and the stuff we did, the better understanding of my own game. Before that, I had no idea what my game was. He gave me that understanding by teaching me how I needed to play. 'This is what we do, and this is why we do it.' He was just a master of seeing things before they would become a problem. So even after a 32-save shutout, he would still say, 'Yeah that was great, but tomorrow we need to do this, because I see that while this is not a problem right now, two or three games from now, you might start getting away from these good habits in these situations.' So we'd go back and fine-tune things and do a couple of focused drills. He did the same thing with Kiprusoff and Nabby, too, so I think all those guys would say the same thing — that he meant a ton to us. In my second year, San Jose assigned me to Manitoba, because I had some success there my first year. To be honest, when they assigned Kenny Wregget there, because Manny Legace beat him out in Detroit, I was like, oh man, I'm not going to play here. But Randy Carlyle told me right away that he didn't care. I was told that I was his guy, and sure enough, I played in a lot of games. I made the All-Star Game that year and gained a lot from that experience, which was fun. I think all of those things combined — the practices, the people you meet, the stuff that you pick up and learn mentally — helps you to be prepared for the playoffs."

Goldman: But it's one thing to do it in the middle of a season, or in the preseason. How did you keep the nerves settled in the elimination games of a grueling playoff series?

Hedberg: "Of course nothing could really prepare me for being thrown into that situation when we got deeper into the playoffs with the Penguins, especially when everything you dream of happens in such a short span. But it was kind of a perfect storm for me; things went well. But you need that luck, too. When you get that break, you need a little luck to really run with it. That's the other thing, too. I mean, I had a good first game against Florida, and because there was a back-to-back in Tampa the next night, I wasn't supposed to play. I'm drained after the game, right? I'm so excited and everything was settling in from the trade and the sudden chance. But they came up to me on the plane and said, 'Johan, you're going tomorrow again. OK, great!' I said. I get to the hotel and I cannot sleep at all. I mean, just nothing. Then I try to go back for a pre-game nap, but can't do it. So I get only a few hours of sleep and I ended up playing a shitty game and losing, 5-1. I was no good at all. Ugh, that was my chance. I blew it. Reporters came up to me and asked what I thought. 'I think I stunk,' I said. 'I'm extremely disappointed. I've been given this chance and I didn't take it and I'm extremely disappointed with myself,' which was the truth. I didn't know this at the time because I got told this many, many years later, but it was one of the best things I could have possibly said [laughing]. Apparently, Pittsburgh's coach picked up the newspaper, saw my quotes, and said, 'You know what? This guy is holding himself accountable. He wants it.' So they loved it, and even though I didn't say anything directly to the coaches, I was just truly devastated. I blew my chance to play in the NHL. But they ended up going back with me and then I won the last seven games leading up to the playoffs. So I was very lucky at that moment, but it was great timing in my life."

Goldman: So you have this unreal push in the playoffs, become a bit of a legend with the Moose nickname and everything else. Then a few years later you went back to Sweden for the Lockout, come back over and play with Vancouver, Dallas, Atlanta, and then New Jersey. What about the different stages of mental growth and maturity throughout your career allowed you to grind it out and be a true asset to all of those NHL organizations?

Hedberg: "I had spent almost three years in Pittsburgh, and then they drafted Marc-Andre Fleury first overall that summer. OK, I thought. I could play with that. I had no problem with it. The same day that I'm about to leave for Stockholm on a flight from Pittsburgh, I get the phone call saying that I had been traded to Vancouver. So I go up there and things started going wrong from Day 1 in Camp. I got hurt just a few days in, and I didn't have Marc Crawford's confidence at all, so it was just a real tough year. That set me back quite a bit, and then the next year after that was the lockout. I went back to Sweden and played there one year, but wasn't really sure if I would get a job in North America, because my numbers were bad, and I just had a shitty year. I ended up signing a deal with Dallas, and they were honest in saying that they just wanted me to back up Marty Turco. I could handle the puck really well, so they thought I would be a great fit because it wouldn't be a big drop-off in that department. I played there one year, but then they said thanks, but we're going to move on. Then I got a chance with Atlanta and I got to play with Kari Lehtonen. Kari was great that first year, he was just unbelievable, and I didn't get to play much at all, just 21 games that year. The next year he ran into some injury problems, so I got more games and things went really well in Atlanta. But even then I can credit that back to my year in Vancouver, because I got to work a lot with Ian Clark. Ian had taught me some stuff that I didn't yet have in my game, especially the movement down on my knees and better patience. I'd say that he really, really prolonged my career. If I hadn't come to work with him, I don't think I would have stayed in the league as long as I did. I think I got better as the years went on, but if I didn't have those good years in Atlanta, I probably wouldn't have had three more years in New Jersey. It has been a long, long road with a lot of interesting things happening along the way for us as a family and me as a player. I'm very blessed to have it all in my memories."

Goldman: Speaking of backing up guys like Marty Turco and Marty Brodeur, can you talk about what type of grind a backup experiences compared to that of a starter? Physically or mentally, what was it like staying prepared behind Brodeur?

Hedberg: "I would come into a new season and people would always ask me how many games I expected to play. They'd say that the backup goalie typically plays six to 10 games. I say, you know what? I don't make predictions. I'm never going to say, 'Oh, I expect to play this many games,' or it's never going to happen. So many things happen to you over the course of a season that you might feel like you're totally out of it for the first few months, and then there's an injury and you end up playing 40 games in a row and go on an unbelievable stretch. So I don't know the answer to this question. I'm just trying to take it day by day. I'm going to prepare the same way whether I'm playing or not, because I never know what's going to happen. I might be in the game after 20 seconds, I might not be in the game at all. But if I do get into a game, I'm going to make sure I'm prepared for it. That also goes back to the Fedyk story and to one I have with Wregget. I remember playing with Kenny in Manitoba, and one time I asked him what he does for a game when he knows he's not playing. 'I prepare the same way regardless, because you never know what's going to happen.' That's another thing I took to heart, and I decided I was going to do that, too. Early in my career, I learned that if I wasn't playing, I would make sure to go on a walk or a run at the mall. If I got thrown into the game and I didn't prepare how I was supposed to, I would be cheating myself and cheating the organization. But I wasn't going to allow that to happen, so I was going to prepare the same way every day. I did that the time I spent backing up Brodeur, and I have to be honest with you, the six games that the reporters talked about became 35 games, because of different injuries and stuff. Never make predictions. Just come in every day with a mindset that you're going to do the right things and that you're going to work. Don't look too far ahead, because you never know what's around the corner."

Goldman: What was the absolute toughest or worst part of your time in New Jersey?

Hedberg: "You know what? I don't think there was a tough part. Every situation has its own challenges and rewards. Obviously, yeah, you're going to get scratched and have to be there for the boys late in practices, and that's a grind on its own. But I enjoyed that stuff. I enjoyed the workouts and everything I got out of it. Mentally, it's a different thing if you're playing 60 games a year or if you're playing 20, for sure. But you go into every game you play thinking that it might be your last. I might be sitting on the bench for 20 days, who knows? If I don't play well, maybe someone else is ready to take this job. You're always playing with a little bit of fear. That's the thing I like to say to myself. I have to perform. If I don't take the chance whenever it comes, you never know when you may get a chance to play again. I talk to a lot of other guys, and that's the way they think, too. When I was in Atlanta, I talked to one of the younger guys one day and he said something like, 'Well it's easy for you guys, you know you'll be here tomorrow.' Actually, no. I don't know. I never tell a guy or let myself believe that I belong here or that I deserve to be in this league. It's such a treat! It's the chance of a lifetime to play in the NHL. If you ever take that for granted, you're in trouble. If you let your guard down, there's someone that wants to take your spot, and I don't want that to happen. Maybe you always need a bit of the fear in your mind that someone might steal your job, so you force yourself to perform day in and day out."

Goldman: So you became comfortable using a little bit of fear as an additional push?

Hedberg: "You could say that, yeah, for sure. Fear might be the wrong word, but in a way it is fear. I think for the long road I had to take to get there in the first place, the severe appreciation I had for being in the NHL was just something I was very proud of. It felt great to come over from Sweden and eventually put on an NHL jersey. I didn't want to lose it for anything in the world. I was going to hang on to it and I was going to do whatever I could to stick around. So yeah, I think fear might be a good word to describe it."

Goldman: I know that language barrier is out there with the rising number of Swedish and Finnish prospects in North America. It's always interesting to see how European goalies comprehend or process certain phrases. It begs the question, do these attitudes and traits you have — the perseverance to embrace the grind for so many years — do you think it's genetic or more a result of your experiences?

Hedberg: "I think for me, I can trace the will I had to win in whatever I did back to a very young age, and to when I first started playing sports. Very early in school, I always wanted to win and I would be extremely upset if I didn't. I played soccer as a child and was always dreaming of being a soccer player. I would be out kicking at the barn door for four hours every day. I always knew I worked harder than all the other kids on my team, but I never really looked at it as work. It was just the one thing that I enjoyed the most. This is what I loved to do. And if I think about how much you actually do train and develop your body just by having fun, it's amazing. We would come home after school, bring our stuff down to the rink, skate for four hours, and then go home. All of the spontaneous sports we played back in the day was great. We all loved it. But I think I had that will to win from the beginning, and that really helped me over the course of my career. I probably wasn't the most talented guy out there, but I think my sheer will to 'make it' was probably pretty high up there. It was my compete level and willingness to do whatever it takes to fulfill the goals. I made it my job and played a long career and that's something I'm extremely happy about. I'm happy that it happened when I was older; I had to develop other parts of my life first. I appreciated it way more than if it would've been given to me. That's what I see with a lot of younger kids. It's given to them at their leisure, so it's something they come to expect instead of appreciate. For me, I'm just happy I got in and found ways to stay there. I think it made me appreciate the grind so much more."

Goldman: Now that you've made the transition into NHL goalie coaching, when you see a young junior prospect that doesn't work hard but clearly has the talent, what do you say to open his or her eyes?

Hedberg: "The first thing I say is easy, because I truly believe it. I believe you play the way you practice. That's how I would approach it with a guy like that. I would say, 'Hey, I don't really see the fire in your eyes here in practice. I think you can do a better job of that. I want you to fight for everything, for every puck. Don't give up. It's going to be good for the guys, it's going to be good for you.' So if you can do that in practice, you're going to do it in games. It's just second nature. Everything we do is repetitive. You have to do it over and over again. If you stand here and don't try or compete on pucks, who's to say that you can just turn it on when the game starts? It just doesn't work that way. Maybe you can do it for one or two games, but you can't do it if you want to have a long career. I think that's probably the most important part of embracing the grind. You have to truly bring it every day."

Goldman: That's a great answer to the book's main question. You just need to work hard every day with a real purpose and put some elbow grease into it.

Hedberg: "And that's regardless of what you do, whether you're in the gym or in the library reading. Whatever you do, you lean into it. I can't remember who told me that, but you lean into it. Just make the most of every chance you get. That's why practice is really important, because it translates into your game. It's good for you, for your satisfaction, and for all of your teammates and family watching. They're going to see how hard you try, and you'll feel some reward from it. They'll say you're good to be around, because you make everybody better. You'll get everyone to work harder. That's a leader — leading by example. You may not have the 'C', but if you're the hardest worker, you'll not only be rising up, you'll bring a lot of other players up with you."

Chapter 20
Write Your Own Story

"To be yourself in a world that is constantly trying to make you something else is the greatest accomplishment." - Ralph Waldo Emerson

Every day is a challenge. Every challenge presents you with a choice. Every choice is a special opportunity to learn more about your purpose and path as a goaltender.

Regardless of age or talent level, you've already faced a number of tough grinds that either thickened your skin and boosted your morale, or pierced your skin and killed your confidence. Through it all, you found a way to persevere and prevail. And by carving your own path and never letting anyone strike you down, you have truly lived.

But knowing that life brings no guarantees, you have to live each day knowing that more wrenches will be thrown your way. Expect the unexpected, because there will always be times where you simply don't get what you deserve. Since this is an inescapable part of the goaltender's struggle, you must always strive to embrace whatever comes next, good or bad, and learn to appreciate that even the darkest days are vital chances to grow and evolve.

More importantly, realize that the lows are as important to your success as the highs. You will always go through times where you're pinned down by unfairness, but you must continue to keep the faith, no matter what. You often hear from coaches and mentors that you get out exactly what you put in. This is true in life and in hockey. So no matter how bad things get, no matter how much your current circumstances grind you down, success has to be earned every day. If you stop working hard when things are at their worst, you'll never make it to the top.

So what type of life do you want to lead? What type of goalie do you want to be? What truly matters to you? Do you accept the responsibility of having to carry a team on your shoulders? Are you willing to admit that you could be working harder? What kind of good habits can you create today to make you a better goalie tomorrow? What can you do to start heading in the right direction? What little habits can you break to keep you from going in the wrong direction?

Just for a second, stop worrying about the little daily problems you face and re-connect with what your heart really wants. Whatever the dream may be, take control of your life, for it's all in your hands! You choose what food you put into your body. You choose your commitment levels in school and on the ice. You choose your friends, and you control the conscious thoughts in your mind. All of these choices not only tip the scales towards happiness and success, but they also play a vital role in molding your personality, priorities, and most importantly, your character.

When dealing with the highs and lows of goaltending, it's also important to realize that it's not just about you, but bringing joy and happiness to others as well. It's not always about "me", because a lot of who you are is also tied to "we" and "team". The more positive and supportive you are towards others, the more it nourishes you and your circle of friends and closest comrades. This creates a healthy and strong support group that every pro goalie cherishes during their career. Without this support group, you are nothing.

The lesson here is that helping people should motivate you, not deflate you, because heeding the call to help others will bring you a certain sense of joy and satisfaction. That alone should give you the inner drive you need to overcome any physical, mental, or emotional grind you might be facing. If you're no longer willing to fight for yourself, at least be willing to fight for those that truly care about you.

A lot of today's sports psychology content focuses on the power of positive thinking, on the "Secret" (otherwise known as the Law of Attraction), and the dangers of bad body language. The reason for this is simple: The way you think defines your reality. You're the unique sum of all your past experiences, thoughts, and actions. Don't weigh yourself down with excess negativity.

So suck it up and don't take it so hard when things goes wrong. This is your life, not someone else's! Do what you love, do it to the best of your ability, and do it consistently. For when tomorrow comes and life goes on, you'll realize that things weren't nearly as bad as they seemed. Even in your worst of times, when the grind has won and you're at a really low point in life, you are still a beautiful, constantly evolving version of you.

No matter which direction life is going, never forget that you still get to write your own story.

Chapter 21

Scott Darling

Introduction: *The personal and emotional demons that Scott Darling has faced over the past five years have been well-documented on an international level. His openness and honesty with everyone he meets has played a vital role in his ability to embrace the grind and rise to stardom with the Chicago Blackhawks. Upon learning of his off-ice struggles, it's impossible to not become a lifelong fan; people everywhere have gleaned inspiration from his fight with alcoholism and stories of his kindness over the past few years have become lore throughout the goaltending community. Having defeated some of the darkest demons an athlete can face, Darling is now out to prove that he's not just a serviceable backup, but capable of being a consistent starter. To know that within four years he went from an SPHL underdog to an NHL backup is almost unfathomable, something that may never be repeated again. Where once there was a stained ring from an empty bottle sitting on his table, now lies the shimmer and sparkle of a beautiful 2015 Stanley Cup championship ring. There may be no better redemption story than this, and we're honored to have him sit down with us in order to share it all with you.*

Valley: If an 18-year-old Scott Darling was sitting across from you at this table right now, what would you tell him?

Darling: "I would punch him in the face. I don't know what I *could* tell him; he didn't listen very well [laughing]. I would probably just tell him to snap out of it, because if you don't stop playing with fire, you're going to make your life a lot harder than it has to be. I think he'd listen to me, but I'm not sure. I'd just tell him that right now, you have no idea what's going to happen. You think you're a big-time draft pick, a high prospect going to a great hockey school. You think you're just going straight to the NHL and never even need to see the American League, let alone the Southern Professional [Hockey] League. Well, two years later, I was begging an SP team to take me on for two hundred bucks a week. It all changed pretty fast, so I'd just tell him to wake up; what you're doing is not working. But if you start doing the right things, life can be great. You don't have to put yourself through any turmoil, and eventually, you will make it to the NHL."

Valley: Can you try and take me through your college experience a little bit?

Darling: "I was recruited to go to Maine and I was supposed to back up Bish [Ben Bishop] my freshman year. It was great meeting him on the recruiting trip and I remember he took me around and showed me a good time. Then I got the news that Bish signed early, so I had a chance to play a lot my first year. We had a really good team with Gustav Nyquist, Brian Flynn, and a few other high-end players. I don't know how or why, but I just wasn't ready for college. I had been living on my own while playing juniors since I was 14, but I think it [college] was all too much for me. The temptation was too great and nobody was there to hold me accountable. I got a taste of that freedom, and in my head, I thought being a goalie at Maine was like being a quarterback at Florida State. I thought I was the big man on campus. I always wanted to party. I had never really worked hard in my life up to that point, and I didn't at school, either. I just got there on my natural ability, so I didn't even know what hard work was all about. Our team was OK and I had spurts of really good stretches my freshman year, but I had no consistency. I could have a shutout one night and get blown out the next night. Then all the stuff away from the rink started catching up to me. I got in trouble a few times — nothing major, just some minor stuff that got my coach's attention. I actually worked pretty hard during the summer between my freshman and sophomore year and got in really good shape, but I didn't change any of my habits away from the rink. I was still partying. Every summer I would train in Boston with Brian Daccord. I've lived out there during the summer since 2007 and that included heading into my second year. It got off to a good start and then the wheels just came off. It was game over the day I turned 21. That happened in December and the next thing I knew, I was off the team and wasn't coming back to school."

Valley: So did they officially kick you off the team?

Darling: "It couldn't be that obvious, because I hadn't actually broken any laws or rules. And if I wanted to stay in school, I could have just stayed as a student and still kept my scholarship. But there was no way I was ever playing hockey there again. I thought everything would be fine and I would just sign with the Coyotes, so I knew I wasn't coming back to Maine by the end of March. That's how quickly it happened, like three months. I finished school that year and never had a problem with grades or anything like that, but in my head, I figured I would somehow magically sign with the Coyotes and everything would be fine. But I didn't put in the work that summer and showed up to training camp without a contract. I hadn't changed any of my habits, so by the end of it [training camp], they pretty much told me that I had to get my shit together. Then they say, 'We're giving you a chance with our East Coast League team, so you're going to Las Vegas.' I showed up in Vegas and kept it together for the first little bit, but I didn't even make it to the regular season. I played one exhibition game, and then one of my old partners in crime came into town with Bakersfield for an exhibition game. We were old friends and teammates, so both of us missed our practice the next day, and both of us got gassed as a result. So here I was, drafted to the NHL in 2007 and committed to Maine and everything was great, and by 2010, I had nothing. No teams, nothing."

Valley: Did your parents know what was going on during those few years?

Darling: "Yeah, they knew. They did everything they could. My dad flew out to Maine one time — I feel bad about it now — just to talk to me about what I was squandering. This was before I got the boot from Maine, and I just wasn't hearing it from him. I couldn't really process what he was saying back then. I remember I called my mom when I was in Vegas one time and said, 'Mom, I need 150 bucks for a flight. Please? There's a team in Louisiana who wants me, I just need to get there.' She was like, 'Are you sure? You should probably just come home, we need to get this figured out.' I said, 'No, I can't. I have to play, I can't miss hockey.' That's how I ended up in the SPHL."

Valley: So you get down to Louisiana, which is also a big party town, and now you're sitting there as a guy who thought he'd be battling for an NHL job to a guy that's just trying to land a job near the bottom of the professional barrel.

Darling: "In a league I used to make fun of when I was playing juniors. My teammates in the USHL and I had this joke back in 2007. We said we're all going to play in the Show and make a ton of money, then we're all going to sign with the Knoxville Ice Bears. This is a joke we actually made so that we could all play together again, because we were such a tight group of guys. I remember that year I was in the SPHL, going to Knoxville and playing against the Ice Bears, then sending all those buddies a photo [laughing]. 'Well, I did it,' I said. 'I'm here. Where are you guys?'"

Valley: Can you remember a defining moment when you finally decided mentally or emotionally to turn things around and seek some help? Did you do that yourself?

Darling: "I knew it for a long time, but I couldn't get over the hump. I don't know why, I just couldn't make the decision. People telling me to get help only pissed me off more and pushed me further in the wrong direction. After the season ended, I was living down in Florida with my uncle in his guest house, just working for him and setting up memorabilia auctions. I was sitting there one day going, 'How did we get here? You don't have a college degree. You don't have any money. You don't even have a team to play for next year.' I basically drank my way out of the SP, even though I was playing fine. My team was bad, but they knew I wasn't there to play hockey. I just needed my 300 bucks a week to get through. It was on July 1, 2011 — that was it for me. I woke up and said enough is enough. I did what I needed to do and turned it all around. I started from the bottom again and slowly chipped away."

Valley: What exactly did that 'chipping away' entail? What was one of the first things you did to begin the turnaround?

Darling: "So my roommate from Louisiana — I don't know if he got traded or just switched teams — moved to the Mississippi RiverKings. I had no credibility or anything at all, so I just remember calling him and telling him I was figuring it out and starting to do the right stuff. I had an agent through all of this, but most of his clients were NHL and AHL prospects, so he didn't really have any connections in the SPHL. But my roommate got me on the team and shortly after that, Mississippi ended up getting a call from my agent. He just wanted to check up on me and make sure there weren't any hiccups. So it all started right there. Then I had to get myself back into shape, because I didn't skate or do anything else that summer except focus on myself. I was like 250 pounds at the start, but I shed the weight pretty quickly. That season, I think I took like seven or eight call-ups. You and Justin know me, I track all the leagues pretty well. I used to have this nightly routine where I'd go home and check every box score from every league and if a goalie didn't finish a game, I'd have my agent call that team. If a goalie got hurt at any level, I knew it would affect the depth charts."

Valley: For sure, it's an opportunity you have to jump on.

Darling: "I'd do it every single night, so I got an obnoxious amount of call-ups. I didn't unpack my bags the whole year. I didn't always play, but it got to the point where I got called up straight to the American League twice from the SPHL, which had never happened before. I went up to Charlotte and Hamilton, Wichita twice, the Florida Everblades twice, and that's all I did the whole year. It kept me busy, kept me interested, and kept me focused on the goal. I wasn't worrying about the rest of it, because that was out of my head by this point. It didn't take too long to make the transformation once I finally made up my mind."

Valley: Everything just started clicking.

Darling: "Even in my social life, it wasn't a temptation anymore. I could go out with my teammates and just tell them I didn't drink. I would even go to the bars with them and drive them around. Yeah, it all just kind of clicked. That year I still played the bulk of my games in the SP, but I made some progress and strides. I got my name back on the map and built some credibility from different coaches that could vouch for me and say I wasn't being an idiot anymore. From there, every summer when I was training in Boston, my agent has a team in this pro training league in Foxborough. We'd play every Wednesday night and I still do it. One night, I was playing against one of the top teams that had like 12 or 13 NHL guys on it, but we won and I played really well. It just so happened that one of the coaches of the Wheeling Nailers was in the crowd, so I ended up signing with Wheeling based on that summer league game. Then they got me the invite to Montreal's camp, but it was during the lockout year, so it was more like Hamilton's camp. Actually, now that I think about it, I caught some really lucky breaks that year that people don't really know about."

Valley: What lucky breaks? What happened?

Darling: "Wheeling shared an affiliation with Montreal and Pittsburgh, but both teams had a fifth goalie signed to an NHL deal — Peter Delmas and Patrick Killeen [respectively]. So when I got there, Wheeling already had two guys with NHL deals set in goal. I was a wreck, every day thinking I was gone at any moment. But Delmas suffered a high ankle sprain during training camp, so he was out the first month of the season, which bought me some more time. Peter got sent down to Wheeling when he returned and I was like, 'That's it, I'm gone. They don't carry three goalies here.' But that night, we played a game and Killeen lost in a shootout, then punched the door to the locker room and broke his hand. It was the same night Peter returned! I would have been sent down the next morning since he had just arrived, but it turned out Killeen was shelved for three and a half months, so I stayed. It was crazy the way it all happened. So It was just Peter and I the rest of the year, and when Killeen's hand healed, I had been playing so well that Pittsburgh actually loaned him to another ECHL team [Orlando Solar Bears]. I ended up finishing that year up with Wilkes-Barre. I didn't play any games for them, but backed up two games during their deep playoff run, and that was that."

Valley: That's incredible. You're walking proof that you almost need to have those small breaks, but at the same time, you can also earn your luck.

Darling: "It happened twice! Once that year, and then again during my year in Milwaukee."

Valley: So after you finish the year with Wilkes-Barre, you go back to train at Daccord's in Boston. Justin told me the story about how you guys met that summer at Merrimack, and how hard you worked when he was there.

Darling: "That's when Mitch Korn signed me to a two-way AHL-ECHL deal with Milwaukee, but I was slated to be the guy in Cincinnati."

Valley: I remember talking to Mitch about that.

Darling: "Throughout this whole thing, I've been a realist. At this point, I was just thrilled to be in the ECHL and not have the fear of being cut every day. I was happy to just be in a system with Mitch, who was great. I actually went down to Nashville a month before camp and skated with Carter Hutton and Pekka Rinne and got to use the Predators training facility, which was just awesome. Working with them was a lot of fun. Then I remember we were in Alaska playing the Aces and I got a call saying that Marek Mazanec couldn't get over the border into Canada, so I had to take the red eye to Abbotsford. I went in and sat on the bench for two games, then went back to Cincinnati and played a few games there, and that's when Peks [Rinne] had his hip injury. So Maz [Mazanec] went up to the NHL and played in close to 20 games, which means I got to move up to Milwaukee for a while. After Peks healed, he suffered the nasty hip infection, which further delayed his return. He was down nearly the entire season, which is why I had such a great opportunity in Milwaukee. When Peks finally got healthy, they sent him to Milwaukee for a conditioning stint, so I had to go back to Cincinnati for a few more games. But at this point, it was deep into the season and it was the best year that I had by far, so they ended up keeping me in Milwaukee and sending Magnus Hellberg down to Cincinnati to finish the year. I only played 26 games in the AHL, but I wasn't planning on getting any to begin with. The fact that I bumped a really good goalie in Magnus down gave me more credibility. My coach wanted to play me more, but he had to develop Preds prospects. I was just happy to get 26 AHL games. The end of that year was the first time I actually had a legitimate shot at an NHL contract."

Valley: Was this the point where you fully believed that you could get there?

Darling: "It was actually before that season started, at Nashville's camp. I didn't know what to expect going into a real NHL mini-camp since I had never been to one before. But with the actual Predators players, I didn't feel out of place in the net. I did feel out of place as a human being, because I was seeing and interacting with these guys for the first time. I had no money and was still chipping away at my own life. But on the ice, I didn't see why I couldn't play there, and I think that gave me a lot of confidence going into the season. Even Barry Trotz gave me 20 minutes in a pre-season game. He said to me, 'I didn't have to do this, but you've been playing well, and I want you to know that you can play at this level.' So that right there was huge; I got to put on an NHL jersey and play one period for the Predators. That really helped me perform during the season. I had the credibility to garner an NHL deal, and through the help of Brian [Daccord], I had met one of Chicago's scouts, a former goalie who I had a pretty good relationship with. I went out of my way to send him a text myself, just letting him know that I was interested. I knew they would need some goalies for the American League, so I wanted to let him know that I was keeping an eye on their depth chart and that I wanted to sign with an NHL team."

Valley: Just that act alone is a great lesson for young goalies. You were proactive on your career. You didn't just sit back and cross your fingers and hope. You were thinking about it every day, looking for gaps in NHL systems, trying to figure out where you could fit in.

Darling: "That's why my agent likes me. I do all the legwork for him, and I still do [laughing]. He just makes the calls. So when I went out of my way, he told me later that he marched right in there and knew the Blackhawks were going to sign me, but he couldn't say anything until July 1. So it all came full circle. It was July 1, three years to the day when I snapped out of it, that I signed with the Blackhawks."

Valley: No way! That is so crazy.

Darling: "Being from Chicago, I was through the roof! I didn't care about the money or anything like that. I would've taken whatever, because I was suddenly slated to be the number-three goalie. Then a few weeks later, I woke up one morning and saw they signed Michael Leighton. Shit! Well, that just bumped me to the number-four spot, so there goes my chance at getting a call-up this year. But I didn't care. I was in the system and knew it would be good to play with a guy like Leighton. He's a legend. So I had a really good camp and later found out that I did a couple of specific things that caught Chicago's eyes. One morning, the coaches were watching us doing some of these footwork drills. I had already been skating for the entire summer because I was so excited, while all the other goalies hadn't put their pads on until camp. So I just looked way faster than everybody else, like I was in mid-season form and they were just getting going. I also did really well in the fitness testing. I almost beat Duncan Keith in the VO2 Max, and nobody had ever come close to him before. They even said they had never seen a goalie test like that. I went down to the AHL before Leighton, but Chicago gave me a full game and I pitched a shutout, then again in a half-game, so I had a great preseason. I went to Rockford and only played in two games before Crow [Corey Crawford] was injured for a couple of days. We were in Toronto at the time, and I remember our equipment guy came up to Michael and I saying, 'Neither of you guys put your laundry in the bin. One of you is going up.' I was pissed at that comment because it got my hopes up, but I knew they were going to call up Leighton, so I literally just threw my stuff down and went and changed. A few minutes later, they brought me into the office and the next thing I knew, I was in a cab heading to Chicago."

Valley: What?! So what's going on inside your head as soon as that happened?

Darling: "I was freaking out! I didn't know what to do. I called my fiancé and my parents and told them I was in a cab heading to the airport in Toronto, and that I was going to Chicago. I got called up and got three starts in a row. I beat Ottawa 2-1, then lost to Anaheim 1-0, then beat Ottawa 5-4 in a shootout."

Valley: OK, time out. You're getting dressed for your first NHL game. You're sitting around looking in the locker room trying to soak it all in. What do you remember most from the big debut?

Darling: "It's funny, because it was so awesome yet so stressful that I don't remember a lot of it. It was a blur. I was obviously really nervous during the day, and I always sleep before a game, but I couldn't sleep at all, so then I was worried about being tired. But adrenaline took over and all the guys were awesome. They're a great group and they made me feel so welcome. The game itself got off to a hot start. I made like seven saves in the first two minutes, including a few big ones right away. The rest of the way felt more like a normal game and we won 2-1."

Valley: So there's 10 seconds left and you're up 2-1 and like any rookie goalie, you're watching the clock and seeing it count down. What on earth is going on in your head?

Darling: "I just couldn't believe it. I was waiting to wake up from a dream. It was crazy."

Valley: So you get off the ice, sit down in your stall, and you're just like...I did it.

Darling: "I didn't sleep at all that night [laughing]. To celebrate, my fiancé and I went back to the hotel and just ordered everything off the room service menu. I mean, we got ice cream and cheeseburgers and just hung out in our robes, feeling fancy in this nice hotel in Chicago. It was funny and we joked about it the whole night. I couldn't believe it actually happened."

Valley: Then you lost a tight 1-0 game against Anaheim.

Darling: "John Gibson pitched a shutout and the one goal I allowed was a short-handed 3-on-0 and it was the ref's fault [laughing]. But I played well. In Ottawa, they put me back in and I played pretty well, but it was a 5-4 win, so obviously it wasn't my best game. I'm feeling pretty high at this point, but Corey was back for that game, so now a decision had to be made between me and Antti [Raanta]. We flew into Toronto and got in around 2:30 in the morning and I'm still grinning walking through the lobby when our hockey ops guy goes, 'Darls, I gotta talk to you.' I walked around the corner and Coach Q [Joel Quenneville] and [goalie coach] Jimmy Waite are standing there, ready to send me down [laughing]. I went from high to low in a hurry, and I don't think I was called back up again until December when I played in four more games because Corey was hurt. Once he got healthy, I was in Rockford for about another month. Then I signed a two-year extension, which was great. I never had a two-year deal before, so I had some job security [laughing]. They called me up the next day and I haven't been back down since."

Valley: Isn't that crazy?

Darling: "It's crazy."

Valley: Then you go on to win the Stanley Cup [laughing]. After everything you've gone through, achieving that is the ultimate dream come true. How was that experience?

Darling: "It was great. It means a lot more to me that I got three of the 16 playoff wins. I feel like the last two years have kind of been an exception to the rule.

This year [2016 Stanley Cup Playoffs] you had Matt Murray, Marc-Andre Fleury, and Jeff Zatkoff playing, but usually it's just one guy all the way through. I didn't touch the ice again after the Nashville series, but it was still so stressful. I don't know if I've ever been that stressed before, and I wasn't even playing. The series against Anaheim was insane. You're just going high-to-low over and over again. I was sitting on the bench just chewing on my fingers for like two months. We pulled out that series, and then the series against Tampa Bay was so tight, but Crow was standing on his head and Kaner scored the second goal in the final game with maybe five or six minutes left. The clock couldn't go any slower. We were all just standing there on the bench, just watching the clock. It was painful. I honestly don't remember a lot of it. I just went nuts."

Valley: So you guys win the Stanley Cup and you go out on the ice and hold that thing above your head. How long did it take for you to sit there and realize you went from the bottom of the barrel in the pro hockey world to the absolute very top, something that few people who ever play the game will ever experience?

Darling: "It took me a couple of weeks. It's so crazy when you win it all. I was the first guy to get the day with the Cup, so I was dealing with that and the parades and all this other stuff right away. But after that, my fiancé and I went on vacation to Mexico and I think that's when it finally settled in, when I was sitting on the beach one day. You think about where you were a couple of years before: I couldn't even afford to put gas in my car and now I'm trying to buy a house in Chicago. Just all of it is so, so crazy."

Valley: Was there any time during your journey when you just wanted to quit?

Darling: "I never came close to quitting. I love being a goalie. I even told my fiancé that I never actually seriously thought I'd make it to the NHL until I was in the American League. In the early part when we were dating, I asked for her thoughts on living abroad, because I figured I would have to go play in Germany or somewhere else in Europe. So that's where my mindset was. I told her I wasn't going to stop playing until they won't let me; I'm going to play until I simply can't anymore. I would've been the guy playing in the SPHL for 15 years, because I just love doing it so much.

It's the best thing ever, and it's what I've known my whole life. It was actually a good thing that I didn't have anything to fall back on when it was looking really grim in Louisiana. I didn't have a college degree and I didn't have any money to go back to school."

Valley: So it became a blessing in disguise that you didn't have anything else.

Darling: "That's why I was able to just put all of my eggs into one basket and grind it out. I think some guys may have the potential to play longer or do better, but if they graduated from Princeton, they could be making a ton of money doing open heart surgeries or something like that. I never thought about quitting, because it was all I had. But some days were really tough."

Valley: It's an unbelievable story that you can't even write. You really can't.

Darling: "People have told me that I need to write a book or sell the movie rights and stuff like that. But I don't know if you could really portray what it was actually like."

Valley: Now that you're in the NHL and you know you belong, the next step is to prove you can be a starter in the League, right? Everyone knows you're now the type of person that trains your butt off to be in a position to take another opportunity when it arises.

Darling: "That's been the motto the past four years. 'Luck is when preparation meets opportunity.' That's what it has been for me. I didn't know when these chances were going to happen, but I didn't botch any of them. It could have gone very differently, but every time I got a chance, I made the most of it."

Valley: Do you see yourself as a mentally tough guy?

Darling: "Some days. I think all of us are in some way, just to do what we do as goalies. I'd say we're definitely mentally tougher than your average person walking around. I don't know if I'm the toughest mentally; sometimes I'm too hard on myself or I get in my own head, but not to the point where it affects my game. It can affect my life, though. Especially being a backup, you don't get to go right back in if you play a bad game. So I can potentially be in a bad mood for two full weeks after playing a bad game, because it's all I think about until I can play again."

Valley: Do you still get nervous?

Darling: "Oh yeah. Actually, I throw up before every game. It started before my first American League game. It never happened before that, but now it happens every game. All of the guys on the team love it. They think it's hilarious."

Valley: That's tough for many people to imagine, but I know how that feels. I would get extremely nervous and then I would get superstitious.

Darling: "I'm not too bad with that stuff. I do a couple of quirky things, but nothing that will stress me out if I didn't drink the right stuff before a game or whatever."

Valley: Ells [Brian Elliott] and I actually talked about this the other day when he spoke at the NetWork Goaltending coaching symposium. When he was preparing for the big Game 7 in Chicago, he said something that helped him — and he actually got this advice from Curtis Joseph — was to be able to say it out loud to himself: "I'm nervous." He was able to say that and accept that it was okay to feel that way.

Darling: "That is a tactic I think I might just do naturally [laughing]. I make fun of myself and just roll with it. Guys will see the nausea on my face and they love listening to me puke, because it's hilarious to them. It's really funny when there's a new guy on the team and he doesn't know about it, because he always asks if I'm OK, and then I just tell him, yeah, I actually feel great now!"

Valley: Does it happen naturally?

Darling: "Yeah. If I don't do it in the locker room, I'll do it on the bench. I've even done it on the ice before."

Valley: How long does it take you to just chill out and play? It can't be easy in Chicago; that anthem gets everyone rocking.

Darling: "I make sure I get everything I need in my body well before, so when I puke, it's just water. It happens after warmups, but it's funny, because I don't like to do it right next to the boys since it's such a disgusting habit. So my trainers are really good at finding me alternate bathrooms and setting me up, because they know it's coming. When we played the Islanders, I had this makeshift walkway to the other bathroom made out of towels, because there's no rubber floor. It was hilarious. But after that I feel really good, so oddly enough it gets me ready to go. Every time I come back into the room, Crawford is always just laughing at me. He thinks it's hilarious."

Valley: How about when you're not starting? Are you still nervous like that?

Darling: "No. I don't get nervous until the other goalie gives up the third goal. I'm really into the games on the bench. A lot of goalies are just out to lunch there, but I'm really into it, and the guys like that about me, because they know they can talk to me about the opposing goalie. That's why guys like Patrick Kane are the best in the world, because they will go the extra mile and ask me questions at practice about why certain shots go in. The best want to know."

Valley: If you have these nerves, when the game was over and you had won, at least for me, it was the best feeling ever. You enjoy it for the night or at least for a few hours, and then you shift your mindset to the next game. But there's no better feeling when the final buzzer sounds and you've won. It's just such a relief.

Darling: "Oh yeah. If you could only bottle that feeling. I can't even put into words how much I love that feeling, but how much I hate the way I feel after losing. I don't even want to be seen. I don't want people to even know I'm alive after a loss. Don't talk to me until the next game. I feel so bad after losing."

Valley: What lessons do you think you've learned mentally about life since your initial breakthrough with the Blackhawks?

Darling: "I've learned a lot about being a pro and what it takes for these guys to do it every day. Just some of the guys on the team — no wonder they're the best in the world. Jonathan Toews and Duncan Keith; they're so consistent with what they eat, what they drink, and how they prepare. I've always done the training on the ice and I work out in the weight room, but that's all I did. I didn't really think about the rest of it. So watching these guys work on the other stuff, like talking to head doctors about focus, has been a great lesson. I also think I've relaxed a little bit more. Seeing these guys actually have two separate lives — their hockey lives and their personal lives — is important. The best guys can leave the game at the rink. I've never really been able to do that, but I think I'm getting better. Especially now that my fiancé lives with me in Chicago, I actually have a home life. Up until this point, I had been all on my own; I was just in survival mode. So that has helped reduce some of the stress and anxiety that comes with being an NHL goalie. I don't think it's a bad thing to have stress, because it means you truly want it."

Valley: It means that you care. It's not really performance anxiety, it's more just that you take it very seriously, because you don't take any of it for granted.

Darling: "Especially being a goalie, you feel responsible for the team. As corny as it sounds, I'm from Chicago and I've been a Hawks fan my whole life, so I feel responsible to do well for the Chicago Blackhawks."

Valley: And you've been on the other side, so you know how quickly things can disappear, too. But you endured and you made it through and the most important thing in life is to be happy, right? Maybe when you were younger, you were having a lot of fun, but you might not have been happy.

Darling: "No, I was definitely not happy."

Valley: Are you at a point now where you can say that you're a happy person?

Darling: "Yeah, for sure. At the end of the day, when you actually take a step back and look at where you're at, this is the greatest job in the world. Literally this is my dream job, and I even have the physical evidence from third grade. A homework assignment asked me what I wanted to be when I grew up, and I answered being a goalie for the Chicago Blackhawks. My grandma kept it. So it's literally all I've ever wanted to do. Like I said before, four years ago, I couldn't even afford to put gas in my car and I could barely feed myself. Now, I have a home. I have a car. I can do stuff. I went to New Zealand this summer. I never thought I would be able to do things like this. From where I was before the transition, I just didn't have the prospect of actually having a good job outside of hockey, let alone inside of hockey. I still get excited about the team's private jet and the nice hotels. Every time I'm at a Ritz-Carleton, I send funny photos to my buddies in the SPHL and we just laugh about it. I've played for so many teams in so many leagues, it's been really fun to joke with my friends and give them an inside look at what actually goes on."

Valley: When Justin and I were talking about the guys we wanted to include in this book, we knew your story had already been well-documented. But at the same time, we wanted to give you that chance to open up and share some of the details and funny stories, because we knew it would be therapeutic for you and really meaningful for readers. I mean "Embracing the Grind" *is* Scott Darling. You are what it is all about. You've gone through every shit storm possible. You've been through every league, through the longest bus trips, through the sleepless nights, you've been through all the torture, but you still love the game. And this leads to my last request. Give a piece of advice to a classroom full of goalies.

Darling: "I want to get across to young people that when you're a teenager, honestly, nothing actually matters. Whatever you're dealing with, whether it's being bullied or not feeling cool in school, or if you're feeling depressed, just try to be a good person. As soon as you go to college and once you're out of high school, it's like a whole new world. It's literally your oyster. You could be the nerdiest kid in high school and rule the world five years later. When you're a teenager, you feel like everything just hurts you so much. You take everything so personally and you feel the need to be socially accepted. I had social anxiety because of all that stuff and that didn't help me at all. It really slowed down my personal development. Looking back on it, what was I even worried about? What was I so uncomfortable about? None of it really matters. Life goes on."

Valley: What you're saying is unbelievable, because you are walking proof that everyone gets to choose their path. At the end of the day, it's up to you to chase down your dreams and make your life whatever you want it to be.

Darling: "When you're a teenager, everything that happens seems so life-altering and dramatic. But at that age, just don't be an asshole, and everything will be fine. You're going to have opportunities to be whatever you want and do whatever you want. It doesn't matter what background you have, who does or doesn't like you, or what part of the country you're from. It's all up to you. Go write your own story."

Chapter 22
Letting Go

At the beginning of our introduction chapter, we shared a few common phrases that people often use to lift themselves up. In our closing chapter, we want to share another motivational quote, but one that can be used to help you let go:

"I've never met someone who could change the past."

Letting go is a vital part of embracing the grind, and learning this lesson begins by understanding that the pitfalls you'll encounter on the goaltending journey can be taken one of two ways — as a positive or a negative. If you take them as a negative, you need to understand that while those times aren't enjoyable, they are still crucial to your overall development.

Every practice, every game, and every conversation with your coaches and teammates is part of who you are and what you ultimately choose to become. Situations can always be interpreted differently, but if you understand that everything you face is part of how you become you, then you're much more likely to have success.

If you have an amazing game, embrace it, then let it go. If you have a tough game, embrace it, then let it go. If you didn't get what you deserved, as much as it hurts, let it go. If you were treated unfairly by a coach or scout, let it go. Holding on to what hurts you is like holding on to a piece of hot coal. The longer you hold it, the more it's going to burn you. The quicker you can understand that and get yourself to forgive, forget, and move on, the easier it will be for you to get through the bad stretches.

Letting go also means learning how to accept a moment for what it is and being ready to accept the next moment with the same openness. Your work ethic, your attitude, and how you prepare are all things you can control. But many of the actual results in a hockey game, like the way the puck bounces and how the game shifts momentum, are not always in your control. So do you have the capacity to realize that you need to be willing to let go and let the game come to you?

Learn how to accept anything and everything that happens, because the more you try to control the results and outcomes of a game or in life, the less control you will actually have.

Every day when you wake up, smile and be thankful that you get to play the great game of hockey. Forget about the past and stop worrying about the future, because in order to reach the top, no matter how easy or hard it is to get there, you must be able to go with the flow.

For as the great Bruce Lee once said:

"You must be shapeless, formless, like water. When you pour water in a cup, it becomes the cup. When you pour water in a bottle, it becomes the bottle. When you pour water in a teapot, it becomes the teapot. Water can drip and it can crash. Become like water, my friend."